Crazy for
BREAKFAST
SANDWICHES

101
Delicious, Handheld Meals Hot
Out of Your Sandwich Maker

Jessica Harlan

Ulysses Press

To Breakfast Clubbers everywhere.

· ·

Published by
Ulysses Press
P.O. Box 3440
Berkeley, CA 94703
www.ulyssespress.com

ISBN: 978-1-61243-370-7
Library of Congress Catalog Number 2014932298

Printed in the United States by Bang Printing
10 9 8 7 6 5 4 3 2 1

Acquisitions editor: Kelly Reed
Managing editor: Claire Chun
Editor: Phyllis Elving
Proofreader: Elyce Berrigan-Dunlop
Design and layout: what!design @ whatweb.com
Cover photograph: © JudySwinksPhotography.com
Food stylist: Anna Hartman-Kenzler

Distributed by Publishers Group West

IMPORTANT NOTE TO READERS: This book is independently authored and published and no sponsorship or endorsement of this book by, and no affiliation with, any trademarked brands of the breakfast sandwich makers or other trademarked brands or products mentioned in this book within is claimed or suggested. Although the recipes in this book were prepared for and tested with one brand of sandwich maker, the recipes can be adjusted appropriately by the reader for use on any brand. All trademarks that appear in this book belong to their respective owners and are used here for informational purposes only. The author and publisher encourage readers to patronize the quality brands and products mentioned in this book.

TABLE OF CONTENTS

INTRODUCTION

Breakfast: The Most Important Meal

I love breakfasts and brunches—everything about them. Savory egg dishes (preferably involving biscuits or a rich hollandaise sauce), cinnamon rolls and other pastries, decadent pancakes or French toast, you name it.

But, like most people, I rarely have time to make the elaborate morning meals of my dreams, even on the weekends. My solution? For a quick and tasty morning meal, I make a sandwich! You can pack a world of flavors alongside an egg between pieces of bread, English muffin, or even bagel. Healthy or decadent, vegetarian or meaty, fancy or lowbrow—the choice is yours.

And never have breakfast sandwiches been easier or more convenient to make thanks to the array of specifically designed cooking tools at your disposal, including egg rings, microwave egg pans, panini presses, sandwich grills, and even all-in-one breakfast sandwich makers. My personal favorite for making these handheld meals—and the one I used to make all the recipes in this book—is the breakfast sandwich maker from Hamilton Beach.

The Hamilton Beach appliance cooks an egg, toasts the bread, melts the cheese, and heats other ingredients at the same time, then assembles the sandwich with the flick of a lever. Another all-in-one machine is the West Bend Egg and Muffin Toaster, which cooks all your ingredients in separate compartments and then allows for easy assembly.

Another way to produce a perfectly proportioned breakfast sandwich is to use a microwave egg pan or a stovetop egg ring, both of which form a perfectly round cooked egg. Progressive International has a microwave version with 2 round compartments for eggs and another section for heating bacon, sausage, or other ingredients, and Nordic Ware offers an Eggs 'N Muffin Pan that heats up your egg and meat together in one pan. Once you have cooked the egg and heated the other ingredients, I recommend putting the assembled sandwich into a panini press or other sandwich grill to toast the bread and melt the cheese.

Since the recipes in this book use the Hamilton Beach breakfast sandwich maker, the egg is placed in the top ring compartment, while the other ingredients of your sandwich are placed in the bottom. With a little tweaking, any of the recipes in this book can be made using one of the round egg cookers and a traditional sandwich press. If you opt for this multi-step approach, feel free to layer the ingredients in whichever order works best for your particular cooker.

The majority of the recipes in this book are for breakfast sandwiches, but once you have a sandwich maker you'll probably want to maximize its use. That's why I've included creations that can be enjoyed any time of day, from lunch to dinner to dessert. For college students, office workers, and others with limited kitchen facilities, I hope this will help you utilize your sandwich maker to its full potential.

The Breakfast Sandwich Through the Years

McDonald's is commonly credited with being the first major restaurant chain to offer a breakfast sandwich: its Egg McMuffin debuted in 1972. The creator of this sandwich was one of the chain's franchisees, attempting to make a handheld version of eggs Benedict. His sandwich was an instant success, and other restaurant chains hastened to create their own handheld breakfasts. Burger King introduced its Croissan'wich about a decade later.

Meanwhile, as people recognized the practicality of a hot, nourishing breakfast that's perfectly portable, breakfast sandwiches started popping up on menus at city diners, coffee shops, and food carts. Today these sandwiches are getting fancy: Starbucks and Panera both offer artisan breakfast sandwiches made with rustic bread and fancy cheese.

The Breakfast Sandwich Kitchen

When you get to be as obsessed with making breakfast sandwiches as I've become, you'll see every other meal as an opportunity to squirrel away a few leftovers to tuck into the next morning's meal. Since you only need an ounce or so of an ingredient for a breakfast sandwich, it makes sense to plan your sandwiches in conjunction with other meals in order to use ingredients wisely.

Here are some tips to help you become a breakfast sandwich pro:

Set aside small amounts of cooked meat and vegetables that would work in a breakfast sandwich. A few stalks of grilled asparagus, a couple ounces of broiled salmon, a slice of steak, a few spoonfuls of cooked corn—these are just a few examples of leftovers that can be incorporated into a breakfast sandwich.

If you're making pancakes or waffles on the weekend, cook a couple just the right size to fit your sandwich maker. We always have a ton of pancake batter left over, and I cook it up in 4-inch rounds to use in sandwiches during the week. Sometimes I'll even sprinkle in cheese or herbs to make savory versions.

Be sure to fully preheat your sandwich maker before using it, so that food cooks thoroughly. I like to plug mine in before I start assembling and preparing the ingredients for my sandwich; usually it's preheated by the time everything is ready to make my sandwich.

I recommend using large eggs in your sandwich maker. Extra-large eggs have the potential to overflow the compartment. I always crack the egg into a small bowl first, giving me more control when I pour it into the sandwich maker. If you're daring, go ahead and crack it right into the top compartment.

Cut or fold foods to fit the sandwich maker. A pair of kitchen shears or an appropriate-size (4 inches in diameter works well) metal biscuit cutter is great for trimming meat, cheese, and bread into rounds.

Precook meat. The top compartment of the sandwich maker gets hot enough to cook an egg, but the bottom compartment doesn't get quite as hot—and certainly not hot enough to cook meat in the short cooking time that's involved. It'll heat meat or melt cheese, but ingredients such as bacon, sausage, and fish should be fully cooked before you put them in the sandwich maker.

Sandwich-Making Tools

You'll find the following tools useful for making the recipes in this book.

Muffin-top pan. This specialized baking pan looks like a muffin pan, but it has wider, shallower indentations (usually about ½ inch deep). I found one with cups the same size as my sandwich maker's compartments (about 4 inches across), and I use it to bake biscuits and other foundations for my sandwiches. A whoopie pie pan is another option, if you can find one with big enough indentations.

Small silicone-coated turning spatula. A mini spatula is just the right size for lifting a piping-hot sandwich from sandwich maker to plate. A plastic or rubbery silicone coating won't scratch the nonstick finish on the appliance.

Custard cup. A little cup or ramekin, big enough to hold about 1 cup of ingredients, is ideal for prepping an egg or mixing up a small batch of ingredients. I buy the glass kind that has a rounded bottom; the shape facilitates thorough mixing.

Biscuit cutter. A round metal biscuit cutter—the kind that looks like a metal ring—is ideal for cutting bread and other ingredients to size. Find one that's as close to the size of your sandwich maker's compartments as possible. Four inches is ideal.

Toaster oven. Some recipes call for small quantities of cooked food, such as biscuits or bacon. A toaster oven is handy so that you don't have to heat up your full-size oven just to make 2 biscuits.

Small skillet. A small skillet—preferably nonstick for easy cleanup—is handy for cooking small amounts of food on the stove before you add them to your sandwich maker. I suggest an 8- or 10-inch size.

Kitchen shears. A clean pair of kitchen shears is useful for cutting ingredients into the right size. I use mine for trimming pancakes and cooked pizza crust.

Sandwich-Making Pointers

After making hundreds of sandwiches, I've picked up a few tricks for producing perfect sandwiches, every time.

When you use softer cheeses, such as Colby or Monterey Jack, it's best to add them to the bottom compartment of the sandwich maker toward the end of the cooking time—especially if they are grated or sliced very thin. Otherwise they'll overcook and become crispy instead of melting.

If your sandwich maker has a nonstick coating (most of them do), you probably won't need to oil it. But for some sticky ingredients, or if you find that your eggs are sticking, the occasional brush of vegetable oil or spritz of cooking spray will help foods release cleanly. A tiny bit of butter can also be brushed or melted onto the compartment, for added flavor.

Bread that's dense or smaller in diameter than the top compartment can sink into the egg, causing an overflow along the edges. While this is mostly an aesthetic matter, you can avoid it by waiting to add the bread until the egg begins to get firm, 2 to 3 minutes.

Let your breakfast sandwich cool for a few moments before eating: the ingredients become very hot!

Tip

Avoid using metal utensils in your sandwich maker—they will damage the appliance's nonstick coating.

The Create-a-Sandwich Chart

On the following pages you'll find 100 recipes for delicious sandwiches—for breakfast and beyond. I hope these recipes will inspire you to experiment with your own concoctions for the sandwich maker. It's as easy as coming up with an exterior (bread) layer and a combination of fillings, spreads, or cheeses to go inside. Use this chart to put together your own creations: pick an ingredient from each column, and you've got your own custom-made breakfast sandwich!

BASE	EGGS	TOPPINGS	SPREADS	MEAT	SEASONINGS AND MIX-INS	SAUCES/ CONDIMENTS
English muffin	Whole egg (size large)	Spinach (raw or cooked)	Cream cheese	Cooked bacon	Minced herbs	Salsa
Bread	2 egg whites	Cheese	Goat cheese	Cooked sausage patty	Dry mustard	Hollandaise sauce
Flour or corn tortilla	¼ cup egg substitute	Steamed asparagus	Artichoke spread	Cooked crabmeat	Grated Parmesan cheese	Tomato sauce
Pancake		Sautéed mushrooms	Tapenade	Cooked ground beef or turkey	Capers	Ketchup
Waffle		Black olives	Pub cheese	Chorizo	Hot sauce	Mustard
Biscuit		Sautéed leeks or onions	Pimento cheese	Canadian bacon	Chopped scallions	Pesto
Crab cake		Tomato slice	Jelly	Veggie sausage	Anchovies	Enchilada sauce
Flatbread		Thinly sliced apples	Ricotta cheese	Prosciutto	Diced jalapeños	Cheese sauce
Pizza				Smoked salmon		
Crumpet						

Chapter One

CLASSIC SANDWICHES AND BEYOND

In this section you'll find all the classic breakfast combinations that most of us know and love. This chapter is a great starting point for getting to know your sandwich maker and perfecting your sandwich-making technique.

EGG *and* CHEESE MUFFIN

It all starts here: the classic, simple breakfast sandwich. Master this and you'll never need to skip breakfast again. Since there are only 3 ingredients, the cheese you use will really make an impact. Choose American cheese for a sandwich that's creamy and mild, or use a sharp cheddar if you want a zestier sandwich.

Makes 1 sandwich

1 large egg
1 English muffin, split
1 slice cheese (about 1 ounce)

1   Preheat the breakfast sandwich maker. Break the egg into a small bowl and pierce the yolk with a fork.

2   Place the bottom half of the English muffin in the bottom compartment of the heated sandwich maker, cut side up; lower the middle plate.

3   Pour the egg into the top compartment and place the top muffin half on the egg, cut side down. Close the sandwich maker.

4   Cook for 4 minutes, or until the egg is set. Carefully open the sandwich maker to place the cheese on top of the muffin in the bottom compartment. Close and cook for 30 seconds more, or until the cheese begins to melt. Slide open the middle plate to assemble the sandwich and remove it from the sandwich maker.

SIMPLE FRIED EGG *on* TOAST

While most recipes in this book call for the egg to be cooked through, including the yolk, sometimes I crave a nice runny, creamy yolk. That's easy to achieve in a breakfast sandwich maker—and you can incorporate this same technique for other open-faced egg sandwiches in this book. Elegant in its simplicity, this super-basic breakfast is immensely satisfying.

Makes 1 sandwich

1 large egg
1 slice bread, lightly toasted
¼ teaspoon butter
1 teaspoon grated Parmesan cheese
Pinch of ground black pepper

1   Preheat the breakfast sandwich maker. Break the egg into a small bowl; do not pierce the yolk.

2   Using a 4-inch round cutter or a knife, cut the bread to fit the sandwich maker. Place it in the bottom compartment of the heated sandwich maker and lower the middle plate.

3   Put the butter in the top compartment and swirl it around to coat the entire base, using a silicone spatula. Pour in the egg, being careful to keep the yolk intact; close the lid.

4   Cook for 2½ to 3 minutes, or until the egg white is completely cooked but the yolk is still soft. Quickly pull out the middle plate to drop the egg onto the toast; remove from the sandwich maker. Sprinkle with the Parmesan cheese and black pepper.

SAUSAGE BISCUIT

Keeping a stash of heat-and-serve sausage patties means you'll always be able to whip up this biscuit sandwich, which is a little more substantial than just a filling of egg and cheese. Vegetarians and health-conscious folks, take note: meatless sausages work very well in this sandwich. I like how the sharpness of cheddar cheese stands up to the spicy biscuit, but of course you can substitute any semi-hard cheese.

Makes 1 sandwich

1 large egg
1 Basic Biscuit, split (recipe on page 98)
1 sausage patty
1 slice cheddar cheese (about 1 ounce)

1 Preheat the breakfast sandwich maker. Break the egg into a small bowl and pierce the yolk with a fork.

2 Place a biscuit half in the bottom compartment of the heated sandwich maker. Place the sausage patty on top of it and lower the middle plate.

3 Pour the egg into the top compartment and place the top biscuit half on the egg. Close the sandwich maker.

4 Cook for 4 minutes. Carefully open the sandwich maker and place the cheese on the sausage in the bottom compartment. Close and cook for 30 seconds more, or until the cheese begins to melt and the egg is cooked through. Slide open the middle plate to assemble the sandwich and remove it from the sandwich maker.

BACON, EGG, *and* CHEESE BAGEL

The bacon-egg-and-cheese combination is another classic. It always reminds me of road trips, because for me many a journey has begun with a stop at our local bagel shop for bacon-egg-and-cheese on a sesame bagel. You can use leftover strips of bacon or make a batch of bacon lattice patties to have on hand for sandwiches. If your bagel is too large for the sandwich maker, use a knife to trim it to fit.

Makes 1 sandwich

1 large egg
1 small or mini bagel, split
2 slices cooked bacon or 1 Bacon Lattice Patty (instructions on page 101)
1 slice cheddar cheese (about 1 ounce)

1   Preheat the breakfast sandwich maker. Break the egg into a small bowl and pierce the yolk with a fork.

2   Place the bottom half of the bagel in the bottom compartment of the heated sandwich maker, cut side up. Arrange the bacon on top of the bagel and lower the middle plate.

3   Pour the egg into the top compartment and place the top half of the bagel on the egg, cut side down. Close the sandwich maker.

4   Cook for 4 minutes, or until the egg is set. Carefully open the sandwich maker and place the cheese on top of the bacon in the bottom compartment. Close and cook for 30 seconds more, or until the cheese begins to melt. Slide open the middle plate to assemble the sandwich and remove it from the sandwich maker.

HAM *and* BRIE CROISSANT-WICH

This sandwich is quick to put together, but it'll add a little bit of elegance and indulgence to your morning—even if you end up wolfing it down while battling traffic on your way to work! I love the flavor combination of spicy mustard, sweet jam, smoky ham, and creamy Brie.

Makes 1 sandwich

1 large egg
1 small croissant
1 teaspoon Dijon mustard
1 tablespoon raspberry jam
1 slice deli ham (about 1 ounce)
1 ounce Brie cheese, sliced

1   Preheat the breakfast sandwich maker. Break the egg into a small bowl and pierce the yolk with a fork. If necessary, use a knife or a 4-inch biscuit cutter to trim the croissant to fit the sandwich maker. Split the croissant in half.

2   In a small bowl, stir together the mustard and the jam. Spread onto the insides of the croissant. Place the bottom half of the croissant in the bottom compartment of the heated sandwich maker, jam side up. Layer the ham and the Brie over the croissant. Lower the middle plate.

3   Pour the egg into the top compartment and gently place the croissant top on the egg, jam side down. Close the sandwich maker, but don't press down if it doesn't close completely.

4   Cook for 4 minutes, or until the egg is set. Slide open the middle plate to assemble the sandwich and remove it from the sandwich maker.

BACON WAFFLE STACK

I was delighted to discover that most frozen waffles are exactly the right size for breakfast sandwich makers! And these days, there are so many options—including multigrain and high-fiber and gluten-free varieties—that waffles can be a healthy choice for yummy breakfast sandwiches. This simple version includes a perfectly shaped bacon patty and a slice of tangy cheddar cheese.

Makes 1 sandwich

1 large egg
2 frozen waffles, thawed
1 cooked Bacon Lattice Patty (instructions on page 101)
1 slice cheddar cheese (about 1 ounce)

1 Preheat the breakfast sandwich maker. Break the egg into a small bowl and pierce the yolk with a fork.

2 Place 1 waffle in the bottom compartment of the heated sandwich maker. Top it with the bacon and lower the middle plate.

3 Pour the egg into the top compartment. Place the second waffle on top of the egg and close the sandwich maker (don't force it if it doesn't close all the way).

4 Cook for 4 minutes. Carefully open and arrange the cheese slice on top of the bacon in the bottom compartment. Close and cook for 30 seconds longer, until the cheese is beginning to melt. Slide open the middle plate to assemble the sandwich and remove it from the sandwich maker.

BENEDICT TO GO

There's something so luxurious about eggs Benedict—the rich, velvety hollandaise sauce and the slab of Canadian bacon. This is certainly not something you could imagine having time to enjoy on a busy weekday morning. But a jar of prepared hollandaise or a packet of the instant kind makes it possible. To make just enough instant hollandaise for a single sandwich, see the note below.

Makes 1 sandwich

1 large egg
1 English muffin, split
1 slice Canadian bacon
1 tablespoon hollandaise sauce (jarred or instant, see below)

1 Preheat the breakfast sandwich maker. Break the egg into a small bowl and pierce the yolk with a fork.

2 Place the bottom half of the English muffin in the bottom compartment of the heated sandwich maker, cut side up. Place the Canadian bacon on the muffin and spread about half the hollandaise sauce on top. Lower the middle plate.

3 Pour the egg into the top compartment. Drizzle the remaining hollandaise sauce over the egg and place the remaining muffin half on top, cut side down. Close the sandwich maker.

4 Cook for 4 to 5 minutes, until the egg is set. Slide open the middle plate to assemble the sandwich and remove it from the sandwich maker.

Tip: SINGLE-SERVE HOLLANDAISE

It's easy to make a single serving from powdered instant hollandaise. In a small, microwave-safe dish, combine 1 tablespoon milk and 1 teaspoon butter. Heat in the microwave at full power for about 30 seconds, or until the butter is melted. Remove and stir in 1 teaspoon powdered hollandaise. Continue to stir until the sauce is creamy and no powdered lumps remain.

THE NEW YORKER

A bagel with lox is a classic New Yorker's breakfast, and this sandwich gives the old favorite a little more substance by adding an egg. I've included my favorite lox accompaniment: capers.

Makes 1 sandwich

1 large egg
1 teaspoon chopped capers
1 small or mini bagel, split
1 tablespoon cream cheese
1 ounce lox (cold-smoked salmon)

1   Preheat the breakfast sandwich maker. Break the egg into a small bowl and whisk with a fork until smooth. Stir in the capers.

2   If necessary, trim the bagel halves with a knife to fit the sandwich maker. Spread with the cream cheese. Place the bottom half in the bottom compartment of the heated sandwich maker, cream cheese side up, and top with the lox. Lower the middle plate.

3   Pour the egg mixture into the top compartment and place the top half of the bagel on the egg, cheese side down. Close the sandwich maker.

4   Cook for 4 minutes, or until the egg is set. Slide open the middle plate to assemble the sandwich and remove it from the sandwich maker.

DENVER OMELET HASH BROWN STACK

With its crisp hash browns and egg layer studded with bell pepper and ham, this meal is an ode to diner breakfasts. It's technically a sandwich, but you'll probably do better eating it with a fork—with a bottomless cup of coffee alongside, of course.

Makes 1 sandwich

1 large egg
1 tablespoon minced red bell pepper
1 teaspoon minced yellow onion
1 tablespoon diced ham or Canadian bacon
2 frozen hash brown patties, cooked according to package directions and kept warm
1 tablespoon grated cheddar cheese
1 tablespoon ketchup

1   Preheat the breakfast sandwich maker. Break the egg into a small bowl and whisk with a fork until smooth. Stir in the bell pepper, onion, and ham.

2   If necessary, use a knife to trim the hash brown patties to fit the sandwich maker. Place 1 patty in the bottom compartment of the heated sandwich maker. Lower the middle plate.

3   Pour the egg mixture into the top compartment. Close the sandwich maker.

4   Cook for 4 minutes, or until the egg is set. Lift the lid and sprinkle the cheese on top of the egg. Close and let cook for 30 seconds more, until the cheese is melted. Slide open the middle plate to assemble the sandwich and remove it from the sandwich maker. Top with the second hash brown patty and add the ketchup.

BREAKFAST BURRITO

Tortillas stuffed with refried beans, egg, cheese, and salsa are a popular breakfast option in the Southwest. When I visit my mom in Santa Fe, this is my favorite way to start the day, so I knew I wanted to create a version for my sandwich maker. If I have black olives or a bit of cooked bacon, ground beef, or turkey on hand, I add that to the bottom part of the sandwich, too. Use a chunky salsa for this burrito, so the sandwich won't get soggy.

Makes 1 sandwich

1 large egg
1 large flour tortilla
2 tablespoons refried beans
1 tablespoon chunky salsa
2 tablespoons grated Colby Jack cheese

1   Preheat the breakfast sandwich maker. Break the egg into a small bowl and pierce the yolk with a fork.

2   Cut 2 rounds from the tortilla to fit the sandwich maker (fold the tortilla in half so you'll only have to cut once). Spread each round with refried beans. Place 1 tortilla round in the bottom compartment of the heated sandwich maker, bean side up. Spoon salsa over the beans and sprinkle with half the cheese. Lower the middle plate.

3   Pour the egg into the top compartment and sprinkle with the remaining cheese. Place the second tortilla round, bean side down, on top. Close the sandwich maker.

4   Cook for 4 minutes, or until the egg is set. Slide open the middle plate to assemble the sandwich and remove it from the sandwich maker.

THE HAWAIIAN

Sweet-tangy pineapple and salty-smoky ham can be a bit of an acquired taste as a pizza topping. On a breakfast sandwich, though, it totally works—especially since a canned pineapple ring and a slice of Canadian bacon fit perfectly between English muffin halves. You can also use a piece of deli ham or a slice of roast ham, but I like the way Canadian bacon is just the right size and shape.

Makes 1 sandwich

1 large egg
1 English muffin, split
1 slice Canadian bacon
1 pineapple ring

1   Preheat the breakfast sandwich maker. Break the egg into a small bowl and pierce the yolk with a fork.

2   Place the bottom half of the English muffin in the bottom compartment of the heated sandwich maker, cut side up. Top with the Canadian bacon and the pineapple ring. Lower the middle plate.

3   Pour the egg into the top compartment and place the top half of the muffin on the egg, cut side down. Close the sandwich maker.

4   Cook for 4 minutes, or until the egg is set. Slide open the middle plate to assemble the sandwich and remove it from the sandwich maker.

Tip

For a delicious twist, add a slice of Swiss or cheddar cheese to the bottom compartment after the egg is set. Cook for 30 seconds more, until the cheese is melted.

GREEN EGGS *and* HAM

This playful sandwich is a favorite with kids. It's inspired by the Dr. Seuss book, of course, so why not serve it on March 2 to celebrate the iconic author's birthday and also National Read Across America Day? I often fix this sandwich in the summer, too, when I'm constantly making pesto with basil from my garden. Feel free to save yourself some work and use store-bought pesto.

Makes 1 sandwich

1 large egg
1½ teaspoons pesto
1 English muffin, split
1 slice Canadian bacon

1 Preheat the breakfast sandwich maker. Break the egg into a small bowl and whisk lightly with a fork. Stir in the pesto until fully mixed.

2 Place the bottom half of the English muffin in the bottom compartment of the heated sandwich maker, split side up; top with the Canadian bacon. Lower the middle plate.

3 Pour the egg into the top compartment and place the top half of the muffin over the egg, split side down. Close the sandwich maker.

4 Cook for 4 minutes, or until the egg is set. Slide open the middle plate to assemble the sandwich and remove it from the sandwich maker.

THE ELVIS

It's said that Elvis Presley's favorite sandwich involved peanut butter, bananas, and sometimes bacon, all fried up in a skillet. I had to try the combination for myself, especially with the bacon (though accounts disagree on whether or not that was actually part of the King's snack). This sandwich doesn't disappoint. When you think about it, it's a pretty filling and nourishing way to start the day: the peanut butter gives you protein, and the bananas are high in potassium and other nutrients; use whole-grain bread for the most nutritional value. The bacon is just there for the yum factor.

Makes 1 sandwich

2 slices white bread, lightly toasted
2 tablespoons peanut butter
1 cooked Bacon Lattice Patty (instructions on page 101)
1 banana, halved crosswise and then sliced in half lengthwise

1 Preheat the breakfast sandwich maker. Using a round 4-inch cutter or a knife, cut the bread into rounds to fit the sandwich maker. Spread each round with peanut butter.

2 Place 1 bread round, peanut butter side up, in the bottom compartment of the heated sandwich maker; cover with the bacon. Lower the middle plate.

3 Arrange the banana slices in the top compartment and cover with the second bread round, peanut butter side down. Close the sandwich maker.

4 Cook for 4 minutes, or until the banana is soft and the peanut butter is gooey. Slide open the middle plate to assemble the sandwich and remove it from the sandwich maker.

STEAK *and* EGGS

Steak and eggs has always seemed like a hungry-man meal. I mean, who really has the appetite to wolf down a T-bone in the morning? (An IHOP menu I came across pairs steak with 3 eggs *and* a stack of pancakes.) This version is a little more manageable. It's a nice way to use a few steak slices left from dinner the night before. For a really elegant twist, sprinkle blue cheese over the steak toward the end of the cooking time.

Makes 1 sandwich

1 large egg
1 teaspoon grainy mustard
2 (4-inch) pancakes (Basic Pancakes recipe on page 102)
2 ounces rare-cooked steak, thinly sliced on the bias

1 Preheat the breakfast sandwich maker. Break the egg into a small bowl and pierce the yolk with a fork.

2 Spread the mustard onto 1 pancake. Place the pancake, mustard side up, in the bottom compartment of the heated sandwich maker. Arrange the steak slices on top. Lower the middle plate.

3 Pour the egg into the top compartment and place the second pancake on the egg. Close the sandwich maker.

4 Cook for 4 minutes, or until the egg is set. Slide open the middle plate to assemble the sandwich and remove it from the sandwich maker.

Chapter Two

MEATLESS MORNINGS

If you're a vegetarian or simply trying to eat less meat, this chapter's for you. The recipes here all rely on the goodness of veggies, cheese, and other ingredients for their yummy flavor and satisfying heft. Indeed, you won't miss the bacon or sausage one bit!

SPINACH *and* SWISS SANDWICH

A handful of spinach is an easy way to bulk up a breakfast sandwich and make it a little more nutritious. Spinach wilts perfectly inside the sandwich maker, requiring no advance cooking. I think nutty Swiss cheese is the perfect complement to the fresh flavor of the spinach.

Makes 1 sandwich

1 large egg
1 English muffin, split
⅓ cup fresh baby spinach
1 slice Swiss cheese (about 1 ounce)

1 Preheat the breakfast sandwich maker. Break the egg into a small bowl and pierce the yolk with a fork.

2 Place the bottom half of the English muffin in the bottom compartment of the preheated sandwich maker, cut side up. Spread the spinach onto the muffin. Lower the middle plate.

3 Pour the egg into the top compartment and cover it with the top half of the muffin, cut side down. Close the sandwich maker.

4 Cook for 4 minutes, or until the egg is set. Carefully open the sandwich maker and place the cheese on top of the spinach. Close and cook for 30 seconds more, or until the cheese begins to melt. Slide open the middle plate to assemble the sandwich and remove it from the sandwich maker.

SAVORY CORN CAKES *with* SALSA *and* PEPPER JACK

This hearty Southwest-style sandwich has a homemade corn cake as its base. It gets a flavor kick with pepper jack cheese and salsa.

Makes 1 sandwich

1 large egg
1 tablespoon chunky salsa
2 cooked Corn Cakes (recipe on page 100)
1 slice pepper jack cheese (about 1 ounce)

1 Preheat the breakfast sandwich maker. Break the egg into a small bowl and pierce the yolk with a fork.

2 Spread salsa on the smooth underside of 1 corn cake. Place, salsa side up, in the bottom compartment of the heated sandwich maker. Lower the middle plate.

3 Pour the egg into the top compartment and place the other corn cake, smooth side down, on the egg. Close the sandwich maker, but don't force the lid down if it doesn't close all the way.

4 Cook for 4 minutes, or until the egg is set. Carefully open the sandwich maker and place the cheese on top of the corn cake in the bottom compartment. Close and cook for 30 seconds more, or until the cheese begins to melt. Slide open the middle plate to assemble the sandwich and remove it from the sandwich maker.

EGG SANDWICH *with* HERBED RICOTTA *and* ARUGULA

Stirring minced herbs into ricotta cheese makes a deliciously creamy spread for a breakfast sandwich. Experiment with different kinds of herbs to find out what flavors you like best. I'm partial to a mixture of parsley and chives, but any leafy herbs—such as cilantro, marjoram, basil, or tarragon—would be nice in this sandwich.

Makes 1 sandwich

2 tablespoons ricotta cheese (whole milk or part-skim)
½ teaspoon minced fresh parsley
½ teaspoon minced fresh chives
⅛ teaspoon garlic powder
Pinch of salt
Pinch of ground black pepper
1 large egg
1 English muffin, split
¼ cup arugula

1   Preheat the breakfast sandwich maker. While it heats, place the ricotta cheese in a small bowl and stir in the herbs, garlic powder, salt, and pepper. Break the egg into another small bowl and pierce the yolk with a fork.

2   Spread the ricotta cheese mixture on the bottom half of an English muffin. Place in the bottom compartment of the heated sandwich maker, ricotta side up, and arrange the arugula on top. Lower the middle plate.

3   Pour the egg into the top compartment and place the other half of the muffin over the egg, cut side down. Close the sandwich maker.

4   Cook for 4 minutes, or until the egg is set. Slide open the middle plate to assemble the sandwich and remove it from the sandwich maker.

SOCAL AVOCADO SANDWICH

This healthy, hearty sandwich reminds me of something you might get in a Los Angeles diner. It's particularly good on slices of dense, homemade multigrain bread, the kind with a ton of chunky seeds and grains mixed in.

Makes 1 sandwich

1 large egg
2 slices multigrain bread, lightly toasted
1 thin slice tomato
⅛ teaspoon hot sauce (such as Cholula)
½ avocado, sliced
1 slice provolone cheese (about 1 ounce)

1 Preheat the breakfast sandwich maker. Break the egg into a small bowl and pierce the yolk with a fork.

2 Using a 4-inch biscuit cutter or a knife, cut the toast into rounds to fit the sandwich maker. Place 1 toast round in the bottom compartment of the heated sandwich maker; top with the tomato slice. Lower the middle plate.

3 Pour the egg into the top compartment, sprinkle with the hot sauce, and top with the second toast round. Close the sandwich maker.

4 Cook for 4 minutes, or until the egg is set. Carefully open the sandwich maker and place the avocado slices and cheese on the tomato in the bottom compartment. Close and cook for 1 minute more, or until the cheese begins to melt. Slide open the middle plate to assemble the sandwich and remove it from the sandwich maker.

SWEET FRUIT BREAKFAST SANDWICH

A touch of maple syrup gives this unusual breakfast sandwich its sweet flavor. It's the perfect antidote to a sugar craving, way healthier than a doughnut or a Danish!

Makes 1 sandwich

1 large egg

1 teaspoon maple syrup

⅛ teaspoon ground cinnamon

¼ teaspoon vanilla extract

2 slices cinnamon raisin bread, lightly toasted

1 tablespoon cream cheese

2 tablespoons diced fresh berries (such as strawberries or raspberries)

1   Preheat the breakfast sandwich maker. While it heats, break the egg into a small bowl. Add the syrup, cinnamon, and vanilla and stir with a fork until smooth.

2   Cut the bread using a 4-inch biscuit cutter or a knife so it will fit the sandwich maker. Spread cream cheese on 1 round and place in the bottom compartment of the heated sandwich maker, cream cheese side up. Sprinkle the berries over the cream cheese. Lower the middle plate.

3   Pour the egg mixture into the top compartment and place the remaining slice of bread on the egg. Close the sandwich maker.

4   Cook for 4 minutes, or until the egg is set. Slide open the middle plate to assemble the sandwich and remove it from the sandwich maker.

PB BP

If you're not in the mood for an egg, this PB BP is just the thing. That's short for Peanut Butter Banana Pancake, and it's snacky and nourishing, gooey and delicious—the perfect way to use leftover pancakes. No pancakes? Try it with whole wheat or cinnamon raisin toast!

Makes 1 sandwich

1 banana
1 tablespoon peanut butter
2 (4-inch) pancakes (Basic Pancakes recipe on page 102)
⅛ teaspoon ground cinnamon

1 Preheat the breakfast sandwich maker. Cut the banana into 3-inch pieces, then halve each section lengthwise into planks. Spread peanut butter on the smooth underside of each pancake.

2 Place 1 pancake in the bottom compartment of the heated sandwich maker, peanut butter side up. Lower the middle plate.

3 Arrange the banana slices in a single layer in the top compartment to cover the surface. (You probably won't need the whole banana; save the rest for another sandwich.) Sprinkle on the cinnamon and then add the second pancake, peanut butter side down. Close the sandwich maker.

4 Cook for 5 minutes, checking after 4 minutes to make sure the pancake doesn't burn. Slide open the middle plate to assemble the sandwich and remove it from the sandwich maker.

Tip: CHOCOLATE PB BP

For a chocolatey variation, top the peanut butter pancake in the bottom compartment with 1 tablespoon semisweet chocolate chips or a 1-ounce piece of chocolate bar. Assemble and cook as for a regular PB BP.

APPLE CHEDDAR BREAKFAST SANDWICH

The combination of sweet apples and tangy cheddar cheese is perfect for a breakfast sandwich, along with an egg and a biscuit or English muffin. Warmed in the sandwich maker, the apple softens just the right amount.

Makes 1 sandwich

1 large egg
1 tart apple (such as Granny Smith)
1 English muffin, split, or 1 Basic Biscuit, split (recipe on page 98)
1 slice cheddar cheese (about 1 ounce)

1   Preheat the breakfast sandwich maker. Break the egg into a small bowl and pierce the yolk with a fork.

2   Using an apple corer, remove the core from the apple. Slice the apple into doughnut-shaped slices, about ¼ inch thick. You'll only need 2 slices for this sandwich; reserve the rest for another use.

3   Place the bottom half of the English muffin or biscuit in the bottom compartment of the heated sandwich maker, cut side up. Layer on 2 apple slices and the cheese. Lower the middle plate.

4   Pour the egg into the top compartment and set the top half of the muffin or biscuit on the egg, cut side down. Close the sandwich maker.

5   Cook for 4 minutes, or until the egg is cooked through. Slide open the middle plate to assemble the sandwich and remove it from the sandwich maker.

CHEDDAR EGGS ON HASH BROWNS

Use prepared hash browns in place of bread for this easy but hearty sandwich. I keep a package of hash brown patties in my freezer and put a few in the oven along with whatever I'm making for dinner, so they're cooked and ready to use the next morning.

Makes 1 sandwich

1 large egg
1 tablespoon grated cheddar cheese
2 frozen hash brown patties, cooked

1 Preheat the breakfast sandwich maker. Break the egg into a small bowl and whisk lightly with a fork. Stir in the cheese.

2 If necessary, trim the hash browns with a knife or a 4-inch round cutter to fit the sandwich maker. Place 1 potato round in the bottom compartment of the heated sandwich maker. Lower the middle plate.

3 Pour the egg mixture into the top compartment. Close the sandwich maker.

4 Cook for 3 minutes, or until the egg is just beginning to set. Open the top compartment and add the second hash brown cake. Close and cook for 1 to 2 minutes more, until the top hash brown is warmed. Slide open the middle plate to assemble the sandwich and remove it from the sandwich maker.

VEGGIE SAUSAGE *on* FRENCH TOAST

Sweet and savory come together in this sandwich, which uses pieces of French toast as its exterior. Frozen veggie sausage patties are a great way to add a little protein to your breakfast. If your bread isn't stale, toast it very lightly to dry it out.

Makes 1 sandwich

2 slices stale white bread
2 large eggs, divided
1 tablespoon heavy cream
⅛ teaspoon ground cinnamon
½ tablespoon butter
2 frozen meatless sausage patties, thawed
1 tablespoon maple syrup

1   Using a 4-inch muffin cutter or a knife, cut the bread into rounds to fit the sandwich maker. In a small, shallow bowl, whisk together 1 egg, the cream, and the cinnamon.

2   Heat the butter in a small nonstick skillet over medium-high heat until melted and foamy. Dip the bread into the egg mixture, then place in the skillet. Cook for 2 minutes, until browned, and then flip over and cook 1 to 2 minutes more. Remove from the pan and transfer to a plate; set aside.

3   Preheat the sandwich maker. Break the remaining egg into a small bowl and pierce the yolk with a fork.

4   Place 1 piece of French toast in the bottom compartment of the heated sandwich maker. Top with the sausage, cutting the pieces to fit if necessary. Lower the middle plate.

6   Pour the egg into the top compartment and cover with the second piece of French toast. Close the sandwich maker.

7   Cook for 4 minutes, or until the egg is set. Carefully open the sandwich maker and drizzle the syrup over the sausage in the bottom compartment. Slide open the middle plate to assemble the sandwich and remove it from the sandwich maker.

ARTICHOKE *and* TOMATO STACK

Artichoke dip is one of my favorite party foods. I think I'd host a shindig just for the opportunity to make it! Not long ago, we miraculously had a bit of artichoke spread left over after a get-together. The next morning, my husband slathered it on English muffins and topped them with poached eggs. It was a fantastic combination, and the inspiration for this sandwich. But don't worry, you don't need leftover artichoke dip in order to make it; I've included instructions for making just enough for 2 sandwiches.

Makes 1 sandwich

1 large egg
1 English muffin, split
¼ cup artichoke spread (or make from recipe below)
1 slice tomato

1   Preheat the breakfast sandwich maker. Break the egg into a small bowl and pierce the yolk with a fork.

2   Cover the bottom half of the English muffin with the artichoke spread and place in the bottom compartment of the heated sandwich maker. Lay the tomato slice on top of the artichoke spread. Lower the middle plate.

3   Pour the egg into the top compartment and place the top half of the muffin on the egg, cut side down. Close the sandwich maker.

4   Cook for 4 minutes, or until the egg is set. Slide open the middle plate to assemble the sandwich and remove it from the sandwich maker.

ARTICHOKE SPREAD

Makes ½ cup

½ cup chopped canned artichokes (packed in water, drained)
1 tablespoon grated Parmesan cheese
1½ teaspoons mayonnaise
Hot sauce, to taste

In a small bowl, stir together the artichokes, Parmesan cheese, and mayonnaise until well mixed. Add a dash of hot sauce to taste. Makes enough for 2 sandwiches.

MUSHROOM *and* LEEK OMELET SANDWICH

I love using leeks in breakfast dishes; they have a sweeter, milder flavor than onions. In this sandwich, the leeks really accentuate the earthiness of the mushrooms, and using a multigrain English muffin gives the sandwich a rustic heartiness. If you wish, you can add a slice of Swiss or Gouda cheese on top of the muffin in the bottom compartment at the end of the cooking time; let it cook for another 30 seconds, or until the cheese begins to melt.

Makes 1 sandwich

1 teaspoon butter
2 cremini or white button mushrooms, minced
1 tablespoon minced leek
Kosher salt and ground black pepper
1 large egg
1 multigrain English muffin, split

1   In a small skillet, melt the butter over medium-low heat. Add the mushrooms and minced leek and sauté, stirring frequently, until the mushrooms soften and the leeks begin to brown. Remove from the heat, season lightly with salt and pepper, and let cool slightly.

2   Preheat the sandwich maker. Break the egg into a small bowl and beat with a fork until the yolk and white have combined. Stir in the mushroom-leek mixture.

3   Place the bottom half of the English muffin in the bottom compartment of the heated sandwich maker, cut side up. Lower the middle plate.

4   Pour the egg mixture into the top compartment and place the top half of the muffin on the egg, cut side down. Close the sandwich maker.

5   Cook for 4 minutes, or until the egg is set. Slide open the middle plate to assemble the sandwich and remove it from the sandwich maker.

CREAMY EGGS *on* CHIVE BISCUIT

I've always loved eggs scrambled with cream cheese and chives, and I created this sandwich as a play on that combination. The cream cheese makes little pockets of creaminess in the egg, and I love the spicy bite of arugula and sharp chive flavor as a nice foil to that. If you already have plain biscuits on hand, just stir a teaspoon of minced chives right into the egg mixture.

Makes 1 sandwich

1 large egg
½ tablespoon cream cheese
1 Basic Biscuit made with chives, split (recipe on page 99)
¼ cup arugula

1 Preheat the breakfast sandwich maker. Break the egg into a small bowl and whisk lightly with a fork. Cut the cream cheese into pea-sized bits and stir into the egg.

2 Set the bottom half of the biscuit in the bottom compartment of the heated sandwich maker, cut side up. Lower the middle plate.

3 Pour the egg mixture into the top compartment and place the other half of the biscuit on the egg, cut side down. Close the sandwich maker.

4 Cook for 4 minutes, or until the egg is set. Carefully open the sandwich maker and arrange the arugula on the muffin in the bottom compartment. Close and cook for 30 seconds more, or until the arugula begins to wilt. Slide open the middle plate to assemble the sandwich and remove it from the sandwich maker.

LEMONY ARTICHOKE-EMMENTALER FLATBREAD

The tangy, fresh flavors in this breakfast sandwich will get your day off to a bright start. For even more flavor, use marinated artichokes—just be sure to drain them well so they don't make your bread soggy!

Makes 1 sandwich

1 large egg
1 piece flatbread or ready-made pizza crust (such as Boboli)
2 canned artichokes (in water), well drained and roughly chopped
1 teaspoon lemon juice
2 tablespoons grated Emmentaler cheese

1   Preheat the breakfast sandwich maker. Break the egg into a small bowl and pierce the yolk with a fork.

2   Using a 4-inch round cutter or a knife, cut the flatbread into 2 rounds to fit the sandwich maker. Place 1 round in the bottom compartment of the heated sandwich maker. Spread the chopped artichokes over the top and drizzle with the lemon juice. Lower the middle plate.

3   Pour the egg into the top compartment and place the second flatbread round on the egg. Close the sandwich maker.

4   Cook for 4 minutes, or until the egg is set. Carefully open the sandwich maker and distribute the cheese on top of the artichokes in the bottom compartment. Close and cook for 30 seconds more, or until the cheese begins to melt. Slide open the middle plate to assemble the sandwich and remove it from the sandwich maker.

MEDITERRANEAN MORNING

Creamy hummus and briny olives make an unexpected filling for a breakfast sandwich that tastes as good in the afternoon as it does in the morning. Try different hummus flavors; I particularly like the roasted red pepper variety.

Makes 1 sandwich

1 large egg
1 pita bread
2 tablespoons hummus
1 tablespoon roughly chopped Kalamata olives

1 Preheat the breakfast sandwich maker. Break the egg into a small bowl and pierce the yolk with a fork.

2 Using a 4-inch round cutter or a knife, cut a pita circle to fit the sandwich maker. Split into 2 layers. Spread the hummus over 1 layer and place in the bottom compartment of the heated sandwich maker. Sprinkle on the olives and lower the middle plate.

3 Pour the egg into the top compartment and cover with the second pita circle. Close the sandwich maker.

4 Cook for 4 minutes, or until the egg is set. Slide open the middle plate to assemble the sandwich and remove it from the sandwich maker.

TAPENADE *and* TOMATO BAGUETTE

Tapenade is a paste of black olives, capers, olive oil, and sometimes anchovies (true vegetarians will want to look for a tapenade without the fish) that gets its name from the word for "capers" in France's Provençal region. This is a great staple to keep on hand—to spread on crackers or bread, to dollop onto cooked fish or chicken, or to use for this delicious sandwich.

Makes 1 sandwich

1 large egg
1 tablespoon butter, softened
2 baguette slices, about ½ inch thick (cut on the diagonal so they fill the compartment)
1 tablespoon tapenade
1 slice tomato
1 tablespoon crumbled goat cheese

1   Preheat the breakfast sandwich maker. Break the egg into a small bowl and pierce the yolk with a fork.

2   Butter 1 side of each baguette piece. Spread the tapenade on the other side of 1 piece and place, buttered side down, in the bottom compartment of the heated sandwich maker. Top with the tomato slice and sprinkle on the goat cheese. Lower the middle plate.

3   Pour the egg into the top compartment. Place the second baguette piece, buttered side up, on the egg. Close the sandwich maker.

4   Cook for 4 minutes, or until the egg is set. Slide open the middle plate to assemble the sandwich and remove it from the sandwich maker.

Chapter Three

HEALTHY STARTS

If you're looking for a lighter, healthier breakfast sandwich, choose one from this chapter. They're designed to add zest and flavor without packing in the fat and calories.

HERBED EGG WHITES *with* TOMATO *and* SWISS

Using 2 egg whites instead of a whole egg for this sandwich shaves off calories and fat. A whole egg averages 3.6 grams of fat, while the white alone has none (but keep in mind that you miss out on some nutrients, such as iron, lutein, and choline). Adding herbs and a super-flavorful cheese makes this sandwich satisfying and substantial. Save the yolks to use in a custard or ice cream.

Makes 1 sandwich

2 large egg whites
¾ teaspoon minced fresh parsley
¾ teaspoon minced fresh chives
1 whole-grain English muffin, split
1 slice tomato
1 thin slice reduced-fat Swiss cheese (about ½ ounce)

1   Preheat the breakfast sandwich maker. Place the egg whites in a small bowl and whisk lightly with a fork. Stir in the parsley and chives.

2   Place the bottom half of the English muffin in the bottom compartment of the heated sandwich maker, cut side up. Arrange the tomato and Swiss cheese on top of the muffin. Lower the middle plate.

3   Pour the egg mixture into the top compartment and place the top half of the muffin on the egg, cut side down. Close the sandwich maker.

4   Cook for 4 minutes, or until the egg is set. Slide open the middle plate to assemble the sandwich and remove it from the sandwich maker.

MULTIGRAIN SANDWICH *with* SPINACH *and* CHEESE

Those little wedges of reduced-fat, spreadable cheese are a great way to enjoy rich creaminess without all the fat and calories of, say, a big wedge of Brie. They're especially good heated, as in this sandwich. My favorite brand is Laughing Cow, and I particularly like the wide range of flavors they offer. Their original Creamy Swiss flavor and Blue Cheese flavor are especially tasty in this sandwich.

Makes 1 sandwich

1 large egg
2 slices multigrain bread, lightly toasted
1 wedge spreadable cheese (about ¾ ounce)
¼ cup fresh baby spinach

1 Preheat the breakfast sandwich maker. Break the egg into a small bowl and pierce the yolk with a fork.

2 Using a 4-inch round cutter or a knife, cut the bread into rounds to fit the sandwich maker. Spread each piece with half the cheese. Place 1 bread round, cheese side up, in the bottom compartment of the heated sandwich maker. Lower the middle plate.

3 Pour the egg into the top compartment and place the other piece of bread, cheese side down, on the egg. Close the sandwich maker.

4 Cook for 4 minutes, or until the egg is set. Carefully open the sandwich maker and distribute the spinach over the bread in the bottom compartment. Close and cook for 30 seconds more, or until the spinach begins to wilt. Slide open the middle plate to assemble the sandwich and remove it from the sandwich maker.

BREAKFAST PIZZA

At an Italian restaurant that we used to frequent for brunch, my husband's favorite menu item was the breakfast pizza. It was just what you'd imagine—pizza with the traditional tomato sauce and melted mozzarella, topped with a fried egg. We've since moved away from that city, and breakfast pizzas are rare on menus in our new neighborhood. So, Chip, this one's for you!

Makes 1 sandwich

1 large egg
Ready-made pizza crust (such as Boboli)
1 tablespoon pizza sauce
1 tablespoon grated part-skim mozzarella cheese

1 Preheat the breakfast sandwich maker. Break the egg into a small bowl and pierce the yolk with a fork.

2 Cut the pizza crust into 2 rounds to fit the sandwich maker. Spread the pizza sauce on 1 of the rounds. Place, sauce side up, in the bottom compartment of the heated sandwich maker. Sprinkle with the cheese and lower the middle plate.

3 Pour the egg into the top compartment and place the second crust round on the egg. Close the sandwich maker.

4 Cook for 4 minutes, or until the egg is set. Slide open the middle plate to assemble the sandwich and remove it from the sandwich maker.

SALSA SCRAMBLE SANDWICH

Add a little zest to your egg with a spoonful of salsa. I like a spicy version to really wake me up, but any variety will do. Choose a chunkier version and drain off the excess liquid so your egg mixture won't be too runny. Using a reduced-calorie English muffin increases the healthy factor.

Makes 1 sandwich

1 large egg
1 tablespoon chunky salsa
1 reduced-calorie English muffin, split

1   Preheat the breakfast sandwich maker. Break the egg into a small bowl and beat lightly with a fork. Stir in the salsa.

2   Place the bottom half of the English muffin in the bottom compartment of the heated sandwich maker, cut side up. Lower the middle plate.

3   Pour the egg mixture into the top compartment and set the top half of the muffin on the egg, cut side down. Close the sandwich maker.

2   Cook for 4 minutes, or until the egg is set. Slide open the middle plate to assemble the sandwich and remove it from the sandwich maker.

Tip

As a variation, try adding a tablespoon of shredded reduced-fat Monterey Jack cheese or a few slices of avocado to the bottom compartment after the egg is cooked. If you add cheese, close the compartment and cook for another 30 seconds or until the cheese begins to melt.

SPINACH *and* FETA OMELET SANDWICH

The combination of spinach and feta cheese is a traditional Greek flavor pairing that works beautifully in egg-based breakfast dishes. With its bold flavor and relatively low calorie content, feta is a great cheese to add to a dish if you're watching your calorie intake: a little goes a long way.

Makes 1 sandwich

1 large egg
2 tablespoons thawed frozen chopped spinach, drained and excess moisture squeezed out
1 tablespoon crumbled feta cheese
2 slices multigrain bread, lightly toasted

1   Preheat the breakfast sandwich maker. Break the egg into a small bowl and pierce the yolk with a fork.

2   Place one piece of bread in the bottom compartment of the heated sandwich maker, top with the spinach and sprinkle with the cheese. Lower the middle plate.

3   Pour the egg into the top compartment and place the other piece of bread on the egg. Close the sandwich maker.

4   Cook for 4 minutes, or until the egg is set. Slide open the middle plate to assemble the sandwich and remove it from the sandwich maker.

GLUTEN-FREE SANDWICH *with* AVOCADO SPREAD

If you're sensitive to gluten, you can substitute gluten-free bread, pancakes, and English muffins in many of the recipes in this book. But when my friend Elizabeth raved about Udi's brand of breads, I decided to buy a loaf and develop a recipe around it. I used Udi's Millet-Chia bread (found in the freezer section) for this sandwich, but any seeded gluten-free bread would be delicious.

Makes 1 sandwich

½ small avocado
1 teaspoon lemon juice
⅛ teaspoon flaky sea salt or kosher salt
2 large egg whites
2 slices seeded gluten-free bread (such as Udi's Millet-Chia bread), lightly toasted

1 Preheat the breakfast sandwich maker. Scoop out the avocado flesh into a small bowl. Mash with the back of a spoon until fairly smooth, then stir in the lemon juice and salt. Place the egg whites into another small bowl and whisk lightly.

2 Using a 4-inch round cutter or a knife, cut the bread to fit the sandwich maker. Place 1 bread round in the bottom compartment of the heated sandwich maker. Lower the middle plate.

3 Pour the egg whites into the top compartment and place the remaining bread round on the egg. Close the sandwich maker.

4 Cook for 4 minutes, or until the egg is set. Carefully open the sandwich maker and spoon the avocado mixture over the bread in the bottom compartment. Close, slide open the middle plate to assemble the sandwich, and remove from the sandwich maker.

Tip

If you have a gluten intolerance, be sure to check the labels of recipe ingredients for hidden sources of gluten. Consult your doctor or nutritionist if you're unsure whether or not you can eat a particular food.

EGG WHITES *with* PESTO *on* BAGEL

Because pesto has such a bold flavor, a little goes a long way. It's delicious in a breakfast sandwich on a chewy bagel.

Makes 1 sandwich

2 large egg whites
1 thin-sliced bagel (or a thinner bagel such as Bagel Thins)
1 tablespoon pesto

1   Preheat the breakfast sandwich maker. Place the egg whites in a small bowl and whisk lightly with a fork.

2   Spread both halves of the bagel thins lightly with the pesto. Place 1 piece, pesto side up, in the bottom compartment of the heated sandwich maker. Lower the middle plate.

3   Pour the egg whites into the top compartment and set the remaining bagel half, pesto side down, on the whites. Close the sandwich maker.

4   Cook for 4 minutes, or until the egg whites are set. Slide open the middle plate to assemble the sandwich and remove it from the sandwich maker.

MULTIGRAIN SANDWICH *with* DILLED COTTAGE CHEESE

Cottage cheese is so underrated! It's a healthy, low-fat way to add a bit of creaminess to a dish, and its mild flavor can be adapted to myriad uses. Here, cottage cheese is mixed with fresh herbs to create a creamy spread that gives this healthy sandwich a little extra bulk. For those who avoid gluten, this sandwich is particularly good made on seeded gluten-free bread.

Makes 1 sandwich

1 large egg
2 tablespoons low-fat cottage cheese
½ teaspoon minced fresh dill
Pinch of kosher salt
2 slices multigrain bread, lightly toasted

1 Preheat the breakfast sandwich maker. Break the egg into a small bowl and pierce the yolk with a fork. In another small bowl, combine the cottage cheese, dill, and salt.

2 Using a 4-inch round cutter or a knife, cut the bread into rounds to fit the sandwich maker. Place 1 round in the bottom compartment of the heated sandwich maker, cut side down, and spoon the cottage cheese mixture over it. Lower the middle plate.

3 Pour the egg into the top compartment and place the other slice of the bread on the egg, cut side down. Close the sandwich maker.

4 Cook for 4 minutes, or until the egg is set. Slide open the middle plate to assemble the sandwich and remove it from the sandwich maker.

PORTOBELLO, EGG, *and* MOZZARELLA STACK

A big, meaty portobello mushroom is the base for a stacked breakfast that's sure to satisfy. Since there's no bread involved, this is a great option for those trying to avoid gluten or carbohydrates.

Makes 1 serving

1 portobello mushroom
½ tablespoon extra-virgin olive oil
Kosher salt and ground black pepper
1 large egg
1 tablespoon grated part-skim mozzarella cheese

1   Using a spoon, remove the stem from the mushroom and scrape away the gills from the underside. Brush both top and bottom lightly with olive oil and sprinkle with salt and pepper. Heat a small skillet over medium heat and add the mushroom. Sauté until softened, turning over halfway through, about 5 to 6 minutes in all.

2   Preheat the sandwich maker. Break the egg into a small bowl and pierce the yolk with a fork.

3   Place the portobello, gill side up, in the bottom compartment of the heated sandwich maker. Lower the middle plate. Pour the egg into the top compartment and close the lid.

4   Cook for 4 minutes, or until the egg is set. Open the lid and sprinkle the cheese over the egg in the top compartment; close and cook for 30 seconds more, until the cheese is melted. Slide out the middle plate to assemble the stack and remove it from the sandwich maker.

TURKEY–EGG WHITE SANDWICH

Lean deli turkey adds protein and substance to this breakfast sandwich. I particularly like smoked turkey in my sandwiches—it tastes almost like bacon!

Makes 1 sandwich

2 large egg whites
1 reduced-calorie English muffin, split
1 teaspoon whole-grain mustard
1 slice deli turkey (about ½ ounce)

1   Preheat the breakfast sandwich maker. Place the egg whites in a small bowl and whisk lightly with a fork.

2   Spread the bottom half of the English muffin with the mustard and place in the bottom compartment of the heated sandwich maker, mustard side up. Arrange the turkey on the muffin, folding it to fit if necessary. Lower the middle plate.

3   Pour the egg whites into the top compartment and place the other half of the muffin over them, cut side down. Close the sandwich maker.

4   Cook for 4 minutes, or until the egg is set. Slide open the middle plate to assemble the sandwich and remove it from the sandwich maker.

Chapter Four

DRESSED-UP BRUNCH SANDWICHES

For a leisurely weekend or a special occasion, these sandwiches have fancier ingredients and slightly more involved preparations. While most of the recipes in this book are for 1 sandwich only, a couple of these sandwiches make 2 servings where it makes sense with regard to ingredients or preparations. Besides, they're too good not to share!

THE MILLIONAIRE

I'm not in the habit of eating caviar for breakfast, but I could get used to this little luxury! I happened to have some caviar and crème fraiche left over after a dinner party in honor of the Sochi Winter Olympics, and my thoughts turned immediately to how good they would taste in scrambled eggs. You don't need the most expensive caviar for these fancy sandwiches; indeed, I found mine for only about $11 for a 1½-ounce jar.

Makes 2 sandwiches

2 large eggs, divided

2 tablespoons plus 2 teaspoons crème fraiche, divided

4 (4-inch) Buckwheat Pancakes, divided (recipe on page 104)

2 teaspoons caviar, divided

1 teaspoon minced fresh dill, divided

1   Preheat the breakfast sandwich maker. Break 1 egg into a small bowl and add 1 tablespoon of the crème fraiche. Whisk until the mixture is smooth and creamy.

2   Stack 2 pancakes in the bottom compartment of the heated sandwich maker and close the middle plate.

3   Pour the egg mixture into the top compartment of the sandwich maker and close the lid. Set the timer for 4 minutes. The egg might puff up like a soufflé while it cooks, which is fine. Don't try to force the lid closed.

4   When the egg is cooked through, open the sandwich maker and remove 1 pancake from the bottom compartment. Close again and slide out the middle plate to drop the egg onto the remaining pancake. Using a spatula, remove and transfer to a plate. Top with 1 teaspoon of crème fraiche, 1 teaspoon of caviar, and a sprinkling of fresh dill. Top with the second pancake.

5   Repeat the process using the remaining egg, 2 pancakes, crème fraiche, caviar, and dill. Serve immediately.

DIXIE BISCUIT

You can't get much more down-South than biscuits, pimiento cheese, and fried green tomatoes. This trio comes together in a fantastic sandwich, which I like to make whenever I have leftover pimiento cheese. But it's easy to whip up just enough cheese spread to make a couple of sandwiches; the recipe is below.

Makes 2 sandwiches

Vegetable oil, for frying
¼ cup coarse dry breadcrumbs (such as panko crumbs)
2 slices green tomato, about ½ inch thick
Kosher salt and ground black pepper
1 tablespoon all-purpose flour
1 large egg white, lightly beaten
2 large eggs, divided
2 Basic Biscuits, split (recipe on page 98)
½ cup pimiento cheese spread (recipe page 54)

1   Pour enough oil into a small skillet to completely cover the bottom by about ⅛ to ¼ inch; heat over medium-high heat. Pour the breadcrumbs into a shallow bowl. Line a plate with paper towels.

2   Season the tomato slices on both sides with salt and pepper. Sprinkle lightly with flour on each side, brush off the excess, and lightly brush with egg white. Dip in the breadcrumbs, pressing so the crumbs adhere; turn over to coat the second side.

3   When the oil is hot (it should shimmer), add the coated tomato slices to the pan. They should sizzle upon contact. Fry until golden brown on the first side, about 3 minutes, and then carefully turn over using a spatula or tongs and fry for 2 to 3 more minutes, until the second side is golden. Transfer to the prepared plate and sprinkle with additional salt.

4   Preheat the sandwich maker. Break 1 egg into a small bowl and pierce the yolk with a fork.

5   Spread the cut side of each biscuit half with about a tablespoon of cheese spread. Place the bottom half of 1 biscuit in the bottom compartment of the heated sandwich maker, cheese side up; top with a fried tomato slice. Lower the middle plate.

6   Pour the egg into the top compartment and place the top half of the biscuit, cheese side down, on the egg. Close the sandwich maker.

7 Cook for 4 minutes. Slide open the middle plate to assemble the sandwich and remove it from the sandwich maker.

8 Repeat, using the other egg and remaining ingredients, to make a second sandwich.

PIMENTO CHEESE SPREAD

Makes ½ cup

¼ cup finely grated sharp cheddar cheese
2 teaspoons jarred diced pimientos, drained
2 tablespoons mayonnaise
⅛ teaspoon hot sauce, or to taste

Combine the cheese, pimientos, and mayonnaise in a small bowl, mashing with a fork or spatula to make a spreadable paste. Season to taste with hot sauce. This makes enough for 2 Dixie Biscuits.

CHICKEN *and* WAFFLES

If you've never tried the strange and wonderful combination of crispy fried chicken and tender waffles, smothered in syrup, you're missing out. It's a soul-food dish that has its roots in Harlem but has been adopted in the South as an honorary regional specialty. Here in Atlanta, we even have a restaurant (owned by singer Gladys Knight) and a food truck devoted to the dish.

In this version, I use round toaster waffles and frozen cooked chicken patties, but you could use leftover homemade waffles, of course. This would also be a great way to use uneaten chicken tenders from a kid's restaurant meal. A note about the syrup: while I'm normally a breakfast snob and will only use the real thing (my husband has gifted me with liters of artisanal maple syrup from Vermont), this dish actually tastes best with the fake stuff.

Makes 1 sandwich

1 large egg
2 frozen toaster waffles, thawed
1 frozen chicken patty or 2 frozen fried chicken tenders, heated
2 tablespoons maple-flavored breakfast syrup

1 Preheat the breakfast sandwich maker. Break the egg into a small bowl and pierce the yolk with a fork.

2 Place 1 waffle in the bottom compartment of the heated sandwich maker; top with the chicken. Lower the middle plate.

3 Pour the egg into the top compartment and place the second waffle on the egg. Close the sandwich maker.

4 Cook for 4 minutes, or until the egg is set. Carefully open the sandwich maker to drizzle the syrup over the chicken in the bottom compartment. Slide open the middle plate to assemble the sandwich and remove it from the sandwich maker.

CIABATTA *with* PROSCIUTTO, EGG, *and* GRUYÈRE

I love breakfasts in French or Italian cafés: the buttery pastries, the big bowls of steaming coffee, the savory sandwiches. I created this sandwich because it seems like something you'd eat while sitting outside a cafe overlooking a Venetian canal. Use the freshest, best-quality bread you can find. The rest of the loaf can be made into French toast, or slathered with butter and jam.

Makes 1 sandwich

1 large egg
2 slices ciabatta or other crusty artisan bread
1 tablespoon butter, softened
1 slice prosciutto (about ½ ounce)
1 ounce Gruyère cheese, sliced
¼ cup arugula

1 Preheat the breakfast sandwich maker. Break the egg into a small bowl and pierce the yolk with a fork.

2 Using a 4-inch round cutter or a knife, cut the bread into rounds to fit into the sandwich maker. Butter 1 side of each round. Place 1 piece, buttered side down, in the bottom compartment of the heated sandwich maker. Drape the prosciutto over the bread and top with the cheese. Lower the middle plate.

3 Pour the egg into the top compartment. Close the sandwich maker.

4 Cook for 2 minutes, or until the egg is starting to set. Open the sandwich maker and place the second bread round, buttered side up, on top of the egg. Carefully add the arugula to the bottom compartment. Close and cook for 2 minutes more, or until the egg is set. Slide open the middle plate to assemble the sandwich and remove it from the sandwich maker.

CRAB *and* LEEK BREAKFAST SANDWICH

Next time you make crab cakes or crab salad, set aside a bit of the crabmeat to make this simple but luxurious little breakfast sandwich. While fresh lump crabmeat is best for this, I've also used canned crabmeat, which is less expensive and easier to keep on hand.

Makes 1 sandwich

1 teaspoon butter
2 tablespoons chopped leeks
2 heaping tablespoons lump crabmeat
½ teaspoon lemon juice
Kosher salt and ground black pepper
1 large egg
1 tablespoon cream cheese
1 English muffin, split

1   In a small nonstick skillet, heat the butter over medium-low heat until it melts and foams. Add the leeks and sauté, stirring frequently, until softened and beginning to brown, about 3 minutes. Remove from the heat and stir in the crabmeat and lemon juice. Season to taste with salt and pepper.

2   Preheat the sandwich maker. Break the egg into a small bowl and pierce the yolk with a fork.

3   Spread the cream cheese on the English muffin halves. Place the bottom half in the bottom compartment of the heated sandwich maker, cream cheese side up. Top with the crab-leek mixture. Lower the middle plate.

4   Pour the egg into the top compartment and place the top half of the muffin on the egg, cream cheese side down. Close the sandwich maker.

5   Cook for 4 minutes, or until the egg is set. Slide open the middle plate to assemble the sandwich and remove it from the sandwich maker.

HERBED PANCAKES *with* PROSCIUTTO *and* EGG

Herb-studded pancakes make a perfect vessel for this simple dressed-up version of ham and eggs. Use the Basic Pancakes recipe and stir in your choice of minced herbs; I like a combination of parsley and chives.

Makes 1 sandwich

1 large egg
2 (4-inch) Herbed Pancakes (recipe on page 102)
2 slices prosciutto (about ½ ounce)

1   Preheat the breakfast sandwich maker. Break the egg into a small bowl and pierce the yolk with a fork.

2   Place 1 pancake in the bottom compartment of the heated sandwich maker; top with the prosciutto. Lower the middle plate.

3   Pour the egg into the top compartment and place the second pancake on the egg. Close the sandwich maker.

4   Cook for 4 minutes, or until the egg is set. Slide open the middle plate to assemble the sandwich and remove it from the sandwich maker.

Tip

If you have some baby spinach or arugula on hand, slip it into the sandwich maker on top of the prosciutto before you slide out the middle plate to assemble the sandwich.

ASIAGO *and* ASPARAGUS FLATBREAD

The next time you roast or grill asparagus, set aside a few spears so you can enjoy this sandwich in the morning. Or keep a bag of frozen asparagus on hand and defrost a few stalks every time you have the craving. (I'm partial to the frozen roasted asparagus sold at Trader Joe's.) You can easily thaw several spears in a covered shallow dish in the microwave on half power for 3 minutes or so.

Makes 1 sandwich

1 large egg
2 pieces flatbread or ready-made pizza crust
2 or 3 spears cooked asparagus, cut into 3-inch pieces
½ ounce Asiago cheese, sliced

1　Preheat the breakfast sandwich maker. Break the egg into a small bowl and pierce the yolk with a fork.

2　Cut the flatbread or pizza crust into 2 rounds to fit the sandwich maker. Place 1 round in the bottom compartment of the heated sandwich maker. Top with the asparagus and layer on the cheese. Lower the middle plate.

3　Pour the egg into the top compartment and cover with the remaining round of flatbread or pizza crust. Close the sandwich maker.

4　Cook for 4 minutes, or until the egg is set. Slide open the middle plate to assemble the sandwich and remove it from the sandwich maker.

CRUMPETS *with* EGGS *and* SMOKED FISH

If you're lucky enough to have a nearby store that sells crumpets, try making this English-inspired breakfast sandwich. Crumpets are similar to English muffins, but their tops are full of craters and you don't split them as you do English muffins.

Makes 1 sandwich

1 large egg
½ teaspoon minced capers
1 tablespoon cream cheese
2 crumpets
1 ounce smoked trout or salmon, broken into flakes

1   Preheat the breakfast sandwich maker. Break the egg into a small bowl and pierce the yolk with a fork.

2   In a small bowl, use a fork to mash the capers into the cream cheese until well mixed. Spread onto 1 crumpet. Place the crumpet, cream cheese side up, in the bottom compartment of the heated sandwich maker. Arrange the smoked fish on the crumpet. Lower the middle plate.

3   Pour the egg into the top compartment and cover with the other crumpet. Close the sandwich maker.

4   Cook for 4 minutes, or until the egg is set. Slide open the middle plate to assemble the sandwich and remove it from the sandwich maker.

CHANTERELLE *and* GRUYÈRE CROISSANT

Rich, buttery, and downright decadent, this sandwich is one to linger over—perhaps with a cappuccino and the Sunday crossword puzzle. If you happen to live where you can forage for chanterelles, this is a really delicious way to use them.

Makes 1 sandwich

½ tablespoon butter
½ cup (about 1 ounce) chanterelle mushrooms cut into 1-inch pieces
Kosher salt, to taste
1 large egg
1 croissant
1 slice Gruyère cheese (about ½ ounce)

1   In a small nonstick skillet, melt the butter over medium heat. Add the mushrooms and sauté, stirring frequently, until their liquid is released and cooks off, about 3 to 4 minutes. Season lightly with salt.

2   Preheat the sandwich maker. Break the egg into a small bowl and pierce the yolk with a fork.

3   Trim the croissant to fit the sandwich maker and split it in half. Place the bottom half in the bottom compartment of the heated sandwich maker, cut side up. Top with the mushrooms, then layer on the cheese. Lower the middle plate.

4   Pour the egg into the top compartment. Close the sandwich maker.

5   Cook for 4 minutes, or until the egg is set. Open the sandwich maker and place the top half of the croissant over the egg, cut side down. Close and cook for 30 seconds more to warm the croissant. Slide open the middle plate to assemble the sandwich and remove it from the sandwich maker.

FRENCH TOAST SANDWICH *with* PRALINE BACON

A sprinkling of brown sugar and pecans does wonderful things to bacon, giving it a salty-sweet, candied quality that's perfect in this French toast–based sandwich.

Makes 1 sandwich

2 slices bacon
1 teaspoon dark brown sugar
2 teaspoons chopped pecans
2 slices stale white bread
2 eggs, divided
1 tablespoon heavy cream
⅛ teaspoon ground cinnamon
½ tablespoon butter

1 Preheat the oven to 400°F. Line a baking sheet with aluminum foil. Following the instructions on page 101, form the bacon into a lattice patty on the prepared baking sheet. Sprinkle with the brown sugar and pecans. Bake for 18 to 23 minutes, until crisp. Transfer to a paper towel–lined plate.

2 Cut the bread into rounds to fit the sandwich maker. In a small, shallow bowl, whisk together 1 egg, the cream, and the cinnamon. Heat the butter in a small nonstick skillet over medium-high heat until melted and foamy. Dip the bread pieces into the egg mixture, then place in the hot skillet. Cook for 2 minutes, until browned, and then flip over to cook the other side, 1 to 2 minutes more. Remove from the pan and place on a plate. Set aside.

3 Preheat the sandwich maker. Break the remaining egg into a small bowl and pierce the yolk with a fork.

4 Place 1 French toast piece in the bottom compartment of the heated sandwich maker. Top with the bacon patty and lower the middle plate.

5 Pour the egg into the top compartment and place the second piece of French toast over it. Close the sandwich maker.

6 Cook for 4 minutes, or until the egg is set. Slide open the middle plate to assemble the sandwich and remove it from the sandwich maker.

BISCUITS *and* GRAVY SANDWICH

My dad is a huge fan of biscuits and gravy; he orders it every time he sees it on a menu (which, in the Midwest town in which he lives, is pretty rare). I wonder if he knows how easy it is to make at home, even when you're just whipping up enough for yourself. This sandwich should satisfy any craving he may have.

Makes 1 sandwich

1 raw sausage patty (about 2 ounces)
1 tablespoon all-purpose flour
½ cup whole milk
¼ teaspoon dried sage
Kosher salt and ground black pepper
1 large egg
1 Basic Biscuit, split (recipe on page 98)

1 In a small skillet over medium-high heat, brown the sausage, breaking it into crumbles with a spoon and cooking it through. Sprinkle the flour over the sausage meat and cook, stirring, for 1 minute, or until the flour is pasty. Stir in the milk and sage and bring to a simmer. Reduce the heat to low and cook until the mixture is thickened, 1 to 2 minutes. Season to taste with salt and pepper.

2 Preheat the sandwich maker. Break the egg into a small bowl and pierce the yolk with a fork.

3 Place the bottom half of the biscuit in the bottom compartment of the heated sandwich maker; spoon the gravy over it. Lower the middle plate.

4 Pour the egg into the top compartment and place the top half of the biscuit on the egg. (If it doesn't fit, wait to add it when you assemble the sandwich.) Close the sandwich maker.

5 Cook for 4 minutes, or until the egg is set. Slide open the middle plate to assemble the sandwich and remove it from the sandwich maker.

CARAMELIZED ONION *and* BLUE CHEESE SANDWICH

Can't decide whether you're hungry for breakfast or for lunch? This sandwich is a good compromise. It's simple to make—especially if you have the onions already prepared—but it has an elegant, complex flavor that seems almost too special for just any old day.

Makes 1 sandwich

1 large egg
1 English muffin, split
1 tablespoon Caramelized Onions (recipe on page 107)
1 tablespoon blue cheese crumbles

1   Preheat the breakfast sandwich maker. Break the egg into a small bowl and pierce the yolk with a fork.

2   Place the bottom half of the English muffin in the bottom compartment of the heated sandwich maker, cut side up. Spoon the onions over the English muffin, then sprinkle with the blue cheese. Lower the middle plate.

3   Pour the egg into the top compartment and place the top half of the muffin over it, cut side down. Close the sandwich maker.

4   Cook for 4 minutes, or until the egg is set. Slide open the middle plate to assemble the sandwich and remove it from the sandwich maker.

BACON, SPINACH, *and* HASH BROWN STACK

A diner-inspired breakfast that's immensely satisfying, this is a perfect cure for what ails you after a late night...perhaps accompanied by a hair-of-the-dog Bloody Mary?

Makes 1 sandwich

1 large egg
2 frozen hash brown patties, cooked according to package directions and kept warm
1 cooked Bacon Lattice Patty (recipe on page 101)
¼ cup fresh baby spinach
Ketchup (optional)

1   Preheat the breakfast sandwich maker. Break the egg into a small bowl and pierce the yolk with a fork.

2   If necessary, use a knife to trim the hash brown patties to fit the sandwich maker. Place 1 hash brown patty in the bottom compartment of the heated sandwich maker and top with the bacon. Lower the middle plate.

3   Pour the egg into the top compartment and close the sandwich maker.

4   Cook for 4 minutes, or until the egg is set. Open the sandwich maker and scatter the spinach over the bacon in the bottom compartment. Close the lid and cook for 30 seconds more, until the spinach is wilted. Slide open the middle plate to assemble the sandwich and remove it from the sandwich maker. Top with the second hash brown patty and add ketchup, if desired.

CRAB CAKE *with* DILLED EGGS *and* HOLLANDAISE

Most seafood departments have ready-made crab cakes that you can take home to cook yourself. I like to pick up a couple for an easy brunch. Add hollandaise from a jar or a powdered mix and you have a meal worthy of any restaurant brunch menu—minus the long wait for a table!

Makes 1 serving

1 large egg
1 teaspoon minced fresh dill, plus more for garnish (optional)
1 prepared crab cake, cooked
2 tablespoons hollandaise sauce*

To make a single serving from a powdered mix, see page 14.

1 Preheat the breakfast sandwich maker. Break the egg into a small bowl and whisk lightly with a fork. Stir in the dill.

2 Place the crab cake in the bottom compartment of the heated sandwich maker. Lower the middle plate.

3 Pour the egg mixture into the top compartment. Close the sandwich maker.

4 Cook for 4 minutes, or until the egg is set. Open the sandwich maker and spoon the hollandaise sauce over the egg. Close and cook for 30 seconds more, until the sauce is warmed. Slide open the middle plate to assemble and remove from the sandwich maker. Sprinkle with minced dill, if desired.

LOBSTER *and* TARRAGON CRÈME FRAICHE MUFFIN

A few chunks of fresh lobster meat can elevate a simple breakfast to the extraordinary. This little meal is a case in point. Tarragon, with its mild, licorice-like flavor, is really wonderful with the lobster, but if you can't find it, dill or chervil makes a good substitute.

Makes 1 sandwich

1 large egg
2 tablespoons crème fraiche
1 teaspoon minced fresh tarragon
1 English muffin, split
¼ cup cooked lobster meat (about 2 ounces)

1   Preheat the breakfast sandwich maker. Break the egg into a small bowl and pierce the yolk with a fork. In another small bowl, stir together the crème fraiche and the tarragon.

2   Place the bottom half of the English muffin in the bottom compartment of the heated sandwich maker, cut side up. Top with the lobster meat. Lower the middle plate.

3   Pour the egg into the top compartment. Close the sandwich maker.

4   Cook for 4 minutes, or until the egg is set. Open the sandwich maker and spoon the crème fraiche mixture over the egg; cover with the top half of the English muffin, cut side down. Slide open the middle plate to assemble the sandwich and remove from the sandwich maker.

SMOKED HAM, PEPPER JELLY, *and* GOUDA BISCUIT

I fell in love with red pepper jelly while developing a recipe for my previous book, *Homemade Condiments*. With its tangy, sweet-and-spicy flavor profile, it is remarkably versatile. I love it in a savory breakfast dish; it adds a bit of sweetness to balance the salty, smoky taste of the ham in this sandwich. You don't need to make your own pepper jelly—you can find it in gourmet food stores, well-stocked supermarkets, or online. Make your own biscuits, or use jumbo-size refrigerator biscuits.

Makes 1 sandwich

1 large egg
2 tablespoons pepper jelly
1 Basic Biscuit, split (recipe on page 98)
1 slice smoked ham (about 1 ounce)
1 slice Gouda cheese (about 1 ounce)

1   Preheat the breakfast sandwich maker. Break the egg into a small bowl and pierce the yolk with a fork.

2   Spread the pepper jelly on the cut side of the biscuit halves. Place the bottom half, jelly side up, in the bottom compartment of the heated sandwich maker. Top with the ham and the cheese. Lower the middle plate.

3   Pour the egg into the top compartment and place the top half of the biscuit, jelly side down, over it. Close the sandwich maker.

4   Cook for 4 minutes, or until the egg is set. Slide open the middle plate to assemble the sandwich and remove it from the sandwich maker.

CORN PANCAKE *with* AVOCADO-CORN SALSA

Here's a fresh, Southwest-style breakfast with just enough heat to wake you up. I like to make this the day after I've served corn on the cob for dinner—I'll cook an extra ear of corn just to have some for the salsa. Otherwise, you can scoop out a couple tablespoons from a bag of frozen corn and defrost it in the microwave.

Makes 1 serving

½ avocado, diced
2 tablespoons cooked corn kernels
1 tablespoon lime juice
1 teaspoon minced jalapeño chile, or to taste
Kosher salt
1 large egg
1 cooked Corn Cake (recipe on page 100)

1   In a small bowl, make the salsa by combining the avocado, corn, lime juice, and jalapeño. Season to taste with salt.

2   Preheat the sandwich maker. Break the egg into a small bowl and pierce the yolk with a fork.

3   Place the corn cake in the bottom compartment of the heated sandwich maker. Lower the middle plate.

4   Pour the egg into the top compartment. Close the sandwich maker.

5   Cook for 4 minutes, or until the egg is set. Slide open the middle plate to drop the egg onto the corn cake; remove from the sandwich maker and transfer to a plate. Top with the avocado-corn salsa.

SMOKED SALMON *and* HASH BROWN STACK

Use hot-smoked salmon (the kind that flakes) for this dish, which is topped with sour cream seasoned with briny capers. You can also use smoked trout. If you make latkes (potato pancakes) for Hanukkah, you might want to save a few to use in place of prepared hash brown patties for these.

Makes 1 serving

1 large egg
1 tablespoon sour cream
1 teaspoon minced capers
1 frozen hash brown patty, cooked
2 ounces smoked salmon or trout

1 Preheat the breakfast sandwich maker. Break the egg into a small bowl and pierce the yolk with a fork. In another small bowl, combine the sour cream and capers; set aside.

2 Place the hash brown patty in the bottom compartment of the heated sandwich maker and top it with the smoked fish. Lower the middle plate.

3 Pour the egg into the top compartment. Close the sandwich maker.

4 Cook for 4 minutes, or until the egg is set. Slide open the middle plate to assemble the stack and remove it from the sandwich maker. Let cool a moment and then top with the sour cream mixture.

Chapter Five

NOT-FOR-
BREAKFAST
SAMMIES

For lunch or dinner, your sandwich maker is a great way to make a quick, single-serving handheld meals.

REUBEN SANDWICH

Legend has it that the Reuben sandwich was invented during a late-night poker game, and the sandwich bears the name of the man who was genius enough to combine corned beef, Swiss cheese, and sauerkraut. For my version, it's easy to mix up a relatively authentic stand-in for the traditional Thousand Island dressing just by combining mayonnaise and ketchup. This sandwich may seem a bit elaborate to make just for yourself, but trust me: it comes together in no time at all, and it's a little luxury that's well worth the effort.

Makes 1 sandwich

2 slices rye bread, lightly toasted
1 tablespoon mayonnaise
1 tablespoon ketchup
¼ cup sauerkraut, squeezed to remove excess liquid
2 thin slices deli corned beef (about 1 ounce)
1 slice Swiss cheese (about 1 ounce)

1 Preheat the breakfast sandwich maker. Using a 4-inch round cutter or kitchen shears, cut the bread to fit the sandwich maker. In a small bowl, mix together the mayonnaise and ketchup. Spread the mixture on the bread.

2 Place 1 slice of bread, dressing side up, in the bottom compartment of the heated sandwich maker. Arrange the sauerkraut on the bread and lower the middle plate.

3 Loosely crumple the corned beef slices to fit into the top compartment of the sandwich maker; top with the Swiss cheese. Place the second slice of bread, dressing side down, over the cheese. Close the sandwich maker.

4 Cook for 4 to 5 minutes, until the cheese is melted, checking to make sure the bread doesn't burn. Slide open the middle plate to assemble the sandwich and remove it from the sandwich maker.

BLACK BEAN BURGER QUESADILLA STACK

A burger with quesadillas for a bun? Why not! This sandwich has the fun elements of Southwest cuisine—melted cheese, spicy black beans, and fresh salsa.

Makes 1 sandwich

2 large flour tortillas
2 tablespoons grated Colby Jack cheese
1 frozen black bean burger, thawed
1 tablespoon chunky salsa or pico de gallo sauce
2 tablespoons shredded lettuce

1   Preheat the breakfast sandwich maker. Stack the tortillas and use a 4-inch round cutter or kitchen shears to cut 2 rounds from the stack, for a total of 4 tortilla pieces. Sprinkle the cheese onto 2 of the rounds, then top with the remaining 2 rounds.

2   Carefully place 1 of the assembled tortilla-cheese rounds in the bottom compartment of the heated sandwich maker. Close the middle plate.

3   Place the black bean burger in the top compartment, followed by the remaining tortilla-cheese stack. Close the sandwich maker.

4   Cook for 2 to 3 minutes, or until the cheese melts. Open the sandwich maker and add the salsa and lettuce to the stack in the bottom compartment. Slide open the middle plate to assemble the stack and remove it from the sandwich maker.

TAMAGO EGG *on* SUSHI CAKES

My husband calls it "dessert sushi"—the sweet egg omelet served at sushi restaurants. It's a great "starter sushi" for those who are new to the cuisine, and a favorite with our kids because of its mild, sweet flavor. True tamago is made by cooking paper-thin layers of sweetened egg, but for this version I've simplified things. For the seaweed component, you can use a piece of nori (look in the Asian section of your supermarket or at an international grocery store), a piece of seasoned seaweed snack (Trader Joe's and Costco are among retailers carrying this addictive treat), or even a generous shake of seasoned seaweed sprinkle.

Makes 1 sandwich

1 large egg
1 teaspoon sugar
Pinch of kosher salt
2 Sushi Rice Cakes (recipe on page 105)
½ small avocado, sliced
1 piece dried seaweed, such as nori, cut to fit the sandwich maker

1   Preheat the breakfast sandwich maker. Break the egg into a small bowl and whisk with a fork until the yolk and white are smoothly mixed. Stir in the sugar and salt.

2   Place 1 rice cake in the bottom compartment of the sandwich maker. Close the sandwich maker and cook for 4 to 5 minutes, until the underside of the rice cake is crisp and lightly browned. Remove and set aside.

3   Place the second rice cake in the bottom compartment and lower the middle plate. Pour the egg into the top compartment. Close the sandwich maker.

4   Cook for 4 minutes, or until the egg is set. Carefully open the sandwich maker and place the avocado, then the seaweed, on top of the rice cake in the bottom compartment. Slide open the middle plate to assemble the sandwich and remove it from the sandwich maker. Top with the other rice cake, crispy side up.

SALMON-RICE STACK

When you have leftover cooked salmon fillet, this handheld lunch or snack is a delicious way to use it. It's a riff on the onigiri rice ball, a popular Japanese appetizer or snack.

Makes 1 serving

½ cup (about 2 ounces) cooked salmon
1 teaspoon seasoned rice vinegar
1 teaspoon sesame seeds
2 Sushi Rice Cakes (recipe on page 105)

1　Place the salmon in a small bowl and break into pieces using a fork. Drizzle with the rice vinegar and sprinkle with the sesame seeds, tossing with a fork to combine.

2　Preheat the sandwich maker. Place 1 rice cake in the bottom compartment and close the sandwich maker. Cook for 4 to 5 minutes, until the underside of the rice cake is crisp and lightly browned. Remove and set aside.

3　Place the second rice cake in the bottom compartment of the sandwich maker and top with the salmon mixture. Lower the middle plate.

4　Place the previously crisped rice cake, browned side up, in the top compartment. Close the sandwich maker.

5　Cook for 5 minutes, then slide open the middle plate to assemble the sandwich and remove it from the sandwich maker.

CHILI CHEESE DOG

A breakfast sandwich maker is a great way to grill hot dogs, cut to fit a burger bun. This is one of my favorite ways to make use of leftover chili.

Makes 1 sandwich

1 hot dog
1 hamburger bun
¼ cup chili
2 tablespoons grated Colby cheese

1　Preheat the breakfast sandwich maker. Cut the hot dog in half crosswise, then split the pieces lengthwise.

2　Place the bottom half of the bun in the bottom compartment of the sandwich maker, cut side up. Spoon the chili over it and lower the middle plate.

3　Arrange the hot dog pieces, cut sides down, in the top compartment. Close the sandwich maker and cook for 5 minutes, until the hot dog is sizzling.

4　Open the top compartment and sprinkle the hot dog with cheese. Place the top half of the bun over the hot dog and cheese, cut side down. Close the sandwich maker and cook for 30 seconds more, until the cheese begins to melt. Slide open the middle plate to assemble the sandwich and remove it from the sandwich maker.

CHICAGO DOG

Chicago-style hot dogs are an unusual breed: ketchup is verboten, but the dog is topped with ingredients you'd never find on any other dog—tomato wedges, a sprinkling of celery salt, and hot peppers. Since this was the hot dog I grew up eating, I couldn't resist including a version here.

Makes 1 sandwich

1 hot dog
1 poppyseed hamburger bun
1 slice tomato
1 dill pickle spear, sliced into pieces
1 tablespoon sweet pickle relish
1 tablespoon diced onion
Pickled hot peppers, to taste
Yellow mustard, to taste
Celery salt, to taste

1   Preheat the breakfast sandwich maker. Halve the hot dog crosswise, then split the pieces lengthwise.

2   Place the entire bun in the bottom part of the sandwich maker. Lower the middle plate.

3   Arrange the hot dog pieces, cut side down, in the top compartment. Close the sandwich maker and cook for 5 minutes, until the hot dog is sizzling.

4   Open the sandwich maker, remove the top half of the bun, and close again. Slide open the middle plate to drop the hot dog pieces onto the bun bottom. Remove from the sandwich maker and add the tomato, dill pickle, relish, onion, peppers, mustard, and celery salt. Cover with the top half of the bun.

BUFFALO CHICKEN SANDWICH

My husband is a big fan of the flavors of buffalo wings: the addictively tangy-hot sauce, the cool blue cheese, and the crunchy celery sticks that always accompany the wings. This sandwich has all these elements, but eating it is a heck of a lot less messy than gnawing on a bunch of chicken wings!

Makes 1 sandwich

1 hamburger bun
1 tablespoon blue cheese crumbles
1 frozen cooked chicken patty, thawed
Hot sauce, as needed (such as Frank's RedHot)
1 tablespoon ranch dressing
1 tablespoon diced celery

1   Preheat the breakfast sandwich maker.

2   Place the bottom half of the hamburger bun in the bottom compartment of the heated sandwich maker, cut side up, and sprinkle with the blue cheese crumbles. Lower the middle plate.

3   Place the chicken patty in the top compartment and sprinkle with the hot sauce. Close the sandwich maker and set the timer for 4 minutes.

4   While the sandwich is cooking, in a small bowl stir together the ranch dressing, celery, and a dash of hot sauce.

5   When the patty is heated through and sizzling, about 4 minutes, slide open the middle plate to drop it onto the bottom half of the bun. Remove it from the sandwich maker. Spread the celery-ranch mixture on the chicken patty and top with the other half of the bun.

CALIFORNIA BURGER MELT

I like to make an extra patty or two when I'm grilling burgers for dinner—they make a quick, easy lunch in the sandwich maker. This fresh-tasting combination always reminds me of Southern California.

Makes 1 sandwich

¼ cup shredded romaine lettuce
1 tablespoon ranch dressing
1 multigrain English muffin, split
1 slice provolone cheese (about 1 ounce)
1 slice tomato
1 cooked burger patty
½ avocado, sliced

1   Preheat the breakfast sandwich maker. Place the lettuce in a small bowl and drizzle with the dressing. Toss to coat, then set aside.

2   Place the bottom of the English muffin in the bottom compartment of the sandwich maker, cut side up. Top with the cheese and the tomato. Lower the middle plate.

3   Place the burger patty in the top compartment; cover with the other half of the English muffin, cut side down. Close the sandwich maker.

4   Cook for 4 to 5 minutes, until the burger is sizzling hot. Carefully open the sandwich maker, add the avocado and the dressed lettuce to the muffin half in the bottom compartment, and close again. Slide out the middle plate to assemble the sandwich; remove from the sandwich maker and cut in half.

MONTE CRISTO *with* RASPBERRY SAUCE

At the diner in my college town, my favorite thing to order during late-night visits was a Monte Cristo sandwich. I loved the custardy French toast exterior, the salty-savory meat and cheese on the inside, and the sweet raspberry dipping sauce. I knew I wanted to try to create it myself—preferably not deep-fried, as I suspect my diner prepared it.

Makes 1 sandwich

1 tablespoon maple-flavored breakfast syrup

1 tablespoon raspberry jam

1 large egg

1 tablespoon heavy cream

⅛ teaspoon ground cinnamon

2 slices stale white bread

½ tablespoon butter

2 slices Gouda cheese (about 1 ounce)

1 slice deli ham (about 1 ounce)

1 slice deli turkey (about 1 ounce)

1 teaspoon powdered sugar

1   In a small bowl, stir together the syrup and the raspberry jam; set aside. In a separate small, shallow bowl, whisk together the egg, cream, and cinnamon. Cut the bread into 2 rounds to fit the sandwich maker.

2   Heat the butter in a small nonstick skillet over medium-high heat until melted and foamy. Dip the bread rounds into the egg mixture, then place in the skillet. Cook for 2 minutes, until browned on the first side, and then flip over and cook 1 to 2 minutes on the other side. Remove from the pan and transfer to a plate; set aside.

3   Preheat the sandwich maker.

4   Place 1 slice of French toast in the bottom compartment of the heated sandwich maker, top with 1 slice of cheese, and then add the ham. Lower the middle plate.

5   Layer the turkey, the other slice of cheese, and second piece of French toast in the top compartment. Close the sandwich maker.

6   Cook for 3 minutes, or until the cheese is melted. Slide open the middle plate to assemble the sandwich and remove it from the sandwich maker. Let cool slightly, then sprinkle with the powdered sugar, cut in half, and serve with the raspberry syrup mixture for dipping.

GRAND CANYON BURGER

In this era of fancy and unusual burgers, I occasionally see them sporting a fried egg on top. It never fails to remind me that this is a favorite burger topping of my friend Kelley (who partnered with me to write the book *Quinoa Cuisine*). I've named this burger after the diner where we used to brunch on Sunday mornings when we both lived in Brooklyn; it was the first place I'd ever seen an egg-topped burger on a menu.

Makes 1 sandwich

1 large egg
1 cooked hamburger patty
1 hamburger bun
Hot sauce, to taste
¼ cup shredded iceberg lettuce
1 slice tomato

1   Preheat the breakfast sandwich maker. Crack the egg into a small bowl. Do not pierce or break the yolk, unless you want it to be cooked through.

2   Place the bottom half of the hamburger bun in the bottom compartment of the sandwich maker, cut side up. Add the hamburger patty, close the sandwich maker, and cook for 2 minutes.

3   Open the sandwich maker and pour the egg into the top compartment. Close the lid.

4   Cook for 2½ to 3 more minutes, until the white of the egg is cooked through but the yolk is still liquid. Slide open the middle plate to drop the egg onto the burger, then remove from the sandwich maker. Top with a dash of hot sauce, the lettuce, the tomato slice, and the top half of the bun.

Tip

Don't forget that you can substitute a turkey or veggie burger for hamburger in any of this book's recipes.

PATTY MELT

I've always loved this retro variation on a burger. In the sandwich maker, it comes out nicely proportioned, with the bread fitting the burger patty perfectly. This is a great way to make use of the Caramelized Onions recipe.

Makes 1 sandwich

2 slices rye bread, lightly toasted
1 slice American cheese (about 1 ounce)
1 tablespoon butter, softened
1 hamburger patty, cooked
1 tablespoon Caramelized Onions (recipe on page 107)

1   Preheat the breakfast sandwich maker. Using a 4-inch round cutter or a knife, cut the bread into rounds to fit the sandwich maker. If the cheese is bigger than the bread rounds, trim it to fit as well. Butter each piece of bread on one side.

2   Place a bread round, buttered side down, in the bottom compartment of the heated sandwich maker. Top with the cheese and the onions. Lower the middle plate.

3   Place the burger patty in the top compartment. Top with the second round of bread, buttered side up. Close the sandwich maker.

4   Cook for 4 to 5 minutes, until the burger is heated through. Slide open the middle plate to assemble the sandwich and remove it from the sandwich maker.

GRILLED CHEESE *and* TOMATO SANDWICH

Serve up this sandwich with a big bowl of tomato soup for a light meal that's sure to conjure up fond childhood memories. While white bread and Swiss cheese are my favorites, you can play around with different types of bread and cheese: try cheddar and rye, for instance, or provolone and whole wheat.

Makes 1 sandwich

2 slices white bread
1 tablespoon butter, softened
2 slices Swiss cheese (about 2 ounces)
1 slice tomato

1   Preheat the breakfast sandwich maker. Using a 4-inch round cutter or a knife, cut the bread into rounds to fit the sandwich maker. Butter each piece on one side.

2   Place a bread round, buttered side down, in the bottom compartment of the sandwich maker. Layer on a cheese slice, the tomato, and the remaining cheese, folding the cheese as needed to fit. Lower the middle plate.

3   Place the second bread round, buttered side up, in the top compartment. Close the sandwich maker.

4   Cook for 3 to 4 minutes, or until the cheese is melted. Slide open the middle compartment to assemble the sandwich and remove it from the sandwich maker. Let cool slightly before cutting in half to eat.

PHILLY CHEESE STEAK SANDWICH

If you've been to Philadelphia, you know how seriously locals take their cheese steak sandwiches, even having specific lingo for ordering the famous treats. While my version is far from authentic, it's got all the trappings of the original. I prefer mine with provolone cheese, but many vendors in Philadelphia offer their sandwiches "whiz wit"—meaning with Cheez Whiz. See the note below to make your sandwich whiz wit.

Notice that this sandwich is made upside down. Turn it over before eating!

Makes 1 sandwich

1 small Kaiser sandwich roll, split
1 slice provolone cheese (about 1 ounce)
2 tablespoons Caramelized Onions (recipe on page 107)
2 slices deli roast beef (about 2 ounces)

1   Preheat the breakfast sandwich maker.

2   Place the top half of the roll in the bottom compartment of the heated sandwich maker, upside down. Layer the cheese and the onions over the roll and lower the middle plate.

3   Arrange the roast beef in the top compartment; top it with the bottom half of the roll, cut side down. Close the sandwich maker.

4   Cook for 3 to 4 minutes, until the cheese melts and the roast beef is heated through. Slide out the middle plate to assemble the sandwich and remove it from the sandwich maker. To eat, turn right-side up.

Tip: WHIZ WIT

To make your sandwich "whiz wit," replace the provolone cheese with 2 tablespoons cheese spread (such as Cheez Whiz), spread inside the top half of the roll. Assemble and cook as directed above.

HAM *and* CHEESE MELT

There's nothing like an old-fashioned ham and cheese sandwich, and my version takes a nod from Cuban *medianoche* pressed sandwiches. The name means "midnight" in Spanish, a nod to this sandwich's popularity as a late-night snack. Make one for a quick lunch; it can even be wrapped in foil to eat on the go.

Makes 1 sandwich

2 thick slices crusty white bread (such as ciabatta)
1 tablespoon butter, softened
1 tablespoon mustard
2 slices Swiss cheese (about 2 ounces)
2 slices deli ham (about 2 ounces)
1 dill pickle, thinly sliced on the bias

1 Preheat the breakfast sandwich maker. Using a 4-inch round cutter or a knife, cut the bread to fit the sandwich maker. Spread each piece with butter on one side and mustard on the other.

2 Place 1 piece of bread, buttered side down, in the bottom compartment of the sandwich maker. Top with 1 slice of Swiss cheese and lower the middle plate.

3 Arrange the ham in the top compartment. Layer on the pickle slices and the second cheese slice. Place the remaining bread round, buttered side up, on top. Close the lid (it's okay to press it down slightly if the bread doesn't quite fit).

4 Cook for 3 minutes, or until the meat is sizzling, the bread is toasted, and the cheese is melted. Slide open the middle plate to assemble the sandwich and remove it from the sandwich maker. Cut in half to eat.

Chapter Six

OPEN-FACED MEALS

You'll probably need a knife and fork to eat these meals –
they're stacks of yummy, melty goodness. Paired with a
green salad, they'd make a perfect light lunch or dinner.

PERFECT TUNA MELT

There's something so comforting about a tuna melt: the combination of hearty English muffin, tangy tuna salad, and gooey cheese has a nostalgic, kid-friendly appeal.

Makes 2 sandwiches

1 5-ounce can chunk tuna, packed in water, drained
1 rib celery, minced
3 cornichons or 1 small dill pickle, minced
1½ tablespoons mayonnaise
½ teaspoon Dijon or yellow mustard
Dash of hot sauce (such as Tabasco or Tapatio)
Kosher salt and ground black pepper
1 English muffin, split
2 slices cheddar, Swiss, or Monterey Jack cheese (about 1 ounce)

1 In a small bowl, combine the tuna, celery, cornichons or dill pickle, mayonnaise, mustard, and hot sauce. Mix with a fork until thoroughly combined. Season to taste with salt and pepper.

2 Preheat the sandwich maker. When it is hot, place half of the English muffin in the bottom compartment, cut side up. Lower the middle plate.

3 Fill a ½-cup measure with tuna salad mixture. Turn out into the top compartment of the sandwich maker, using a fork or a small spatula to spread it. Place 1 cheese slice on top of the tuna, folding in the corners to fit if necessary. Close the sandwich maker and set a timer for 3 minutes.

4 After 3 minutes, check the top compartment to make sure the cheese is completely melted. Slide open the middle plate to drop the tuna layer onto the English muffin; remove the sandwich using a turning spatula.

5 Repeat with the remaining muffin half, tuna mixture, and cheese slice to make a second tuna melt sandwich.

ENGLISH MUFFIN PIZZA

One of the first recipes I developed, at the tender age of 8 or 9, was the English muffin pizza. Of course, you probably wouldn't want to taste that early version—it involved ketchup, whatever cheese we happened to have on hand (usually Muenster or American), and a microwave. But it was my favorite snack for years, probably in large part because of the pride I felt in making it myself.

The sandwich maker produces far better results than a microwave—it gets all the ingredients warm and toasty, browns the cheese just enough, and keeps the muffin crisp. And using pizza sauce rather than ketchup makes it taste just like the real thing!

Makes 2 servings

1 English muffin, split
2 tablespoons pizza sauce
8 slices pepperoni
¼ cup grated mozzarella cheese
Italian seasoning or dried oregano

1   Preheat the sandwich maker.

2   On half of the English muffin, spread 1 tablespoon pizza sauce. Arrange 4 pepperoni slices over the sauce. Place half the mozzarella cheese on top and sprinkle lightly with Italian seasoning or oregano.

3   Place the pizza in the bottom half of the sandwich maker. Close the sandwich maker and cook for 3 minutes, or until the cheese is melted on top and starting to brown. Remove with a lifting spatula.

4   Repeat the steps to make a second muffin pizza, using the second muffin half and the other remaining ingredients. Serve immediately.

MINI MARGHERITA

This little pizza is an excellent snack to make in summer, when tomatoes and basil are at their peak. Use a prebaked pizza crust, such as Boboli—you'll be able to cut several rounds from a single crust. The tiny fresh mozzarella balls called *bocconcini* are perfect for this recipe. You'll find them in plastic tubs in the specialty cheese department of your grocery store.

If you wish, you can make 2 of these pizzas at the same time. Just double the ingredients and use both the top and bottom compartments of the sandwich maker.

Makes 1 serving

Ready-made pizza crust (such as Boboli)
2 cherry tomatoes, thinly sliced
1 ounce fresh mozzarella, cut into small chunks
4 basil leaves, cut into thin strips (see note)
½ teaspoon extra-virgin olive oil
Sea salt and ground black pepper

1 Preheat the breakfast sandwich maker.

2 Using a 4-inch round cutter or a knife, cut a round of pizza crust to fit the sandwich maker. Arrange the tomato and mozzarella pieces on the crust. Sprinkle with the basil and drizzle with the olive oil.

3 Place the mini pizza in the bottom compartment of the sandwich maker. Close and cook for 3 minutes, until the cheese is melted and the tomatoes are softened. Open the sandwich maker, remove the pizza, and sprinkle with salt and pepper.

Tip: CUTTING BASIL STRIPS

To cut large leaves such as basil into strips (called a "chiffonade"), stack a few of them on top of each other and roll from the long side into a cigar shape. Using a very sharp knife, cut across the roll to create thin strips.

PORTOBELLO, POLENTA, *and* MANCHEGO STACK

Having a dinner party, and one of the guests you've invited is a vegetarian? No problem! Make this delicious layered dish—it has an elegant look and is hearty and satisfying enough to serve as a main course. I use prepared polenta that comes in a tube, but you could also form homemade polenta (or even grits!) into a patty and chill until firm (see recipe on page 108).

Makes 1 serving

1 portobello mushroom
1 tablespoon extra-virgin olive oil
Kosher salt and ground black pepper
1 slice prepared polenta, ½ inch thick
1 ounce Manchego cheese, sliced

1   Using a spoon, remove the stem from the mushroom and scrape away the gills from the underside. Brush both top and bottom lightly with olive oil and sprinkle with salt and pepper. Heat a small skillet over medium heat and add the mushroom. Sauté until softened, turning over halfway through, about 5 to 6 minutes in all.

2   Preheat the sandwich maker. Brush the polenta slice lightly with the remaining oil and season with salt and pepper.

3   Place the portobello, gill side up, in the bottom compartment of the sandwich maker. Lower the middle plate.

4   Put the polenta in the top compartment. Close the lid and cook for 2 minutes to lightly toast, then flip the polenta over, top with the cheese, and cook 2 minutes more, until the cheese is melted. Slide the middle plate out to assemble the stack and remove it from the sandwich maker.

SHRIMP *and* GRITS STACK

Since shrimp require such a short cooking time, they're ideal for a breakfast sandwich maker. My version is a fun, easy update on the Southern classic.

Makes 1 serving

4 to 5 raw medium shrimp, peeled, cleaned, tails removed
1 tablespoon diced roasted red peppers
¼ teaspoon seafood seasoning (such as Old Bay)
1 cooked Grit Cake (recipe on page 108)
½ tablespoon butter

1   Preheat the breakfast sandwich maker. Place the shrimp in a small bowl, add the red peppers, and sprinkle with the seafood seasoning. Toss with a fork to coat.

2   Place the grit cake in the bottom compartment of the heated sandwich maker. Lower the middle plate.

3   Melt the butter in the top compartment, using a silicone spatula to swirl it around and coat the entire surface. Add the shrimp and close the sandwich maker.

4   Cook for 2 to 3 minutes, or until the shrimp are opaque and cooked through. Slide open the middle plate to drop the shrimp onto the grit cake and remove it from the sandwich maker.

PESTO PIZZA MELT

Homemade or store-bought pesto makes a fresh-flavored topping for this mini pizza. Using a prebaked pizza crust (I like Boboli) means it's super-easy to put together. For a fancier version, replace the grated mozzarella cheese with chunks of fresh mozzarella, the kind that comes in a tub of water.

Makes 1 serving

Ready-made pizza crust (such as Boboli)
2 tablespoons pesto
1 tablespoon roughly chopped Kalamata olives
2 cherry tomatoes, thinly sliced
2 tablespoons grated mozzarella cheese
Sea salt and ground black pepper

1   Preheat the breakfast sandwich maker.

2   With a round cutter or a knife, cut a round from the pizza crust to fit the sandwich maker. Spread the pesto over the crust, then top with the olives, tomatoes, and cheese. Place in the bottom compartment and close the sandwich maker.

3   Cook for 3 minutes, until the cheese is melted and the tomatoes are softened. Remove from the sandwich maker and sprinkle with salt and pepper.

POLENTA PESTO ROUNDS

These little rounds make a tasty snack or appetizer—and since you can make one in each compartment of the sandwich maker, there's enough to share! Use slices from a tube of store-bought polenta, or make your own polenta cakes following the instructions on page 108.

Makes 2 servings

2 slices or patties prepared polenta, about ½ inch thick
Olive oil for brushing
Salt and ground black pepper
2 tablespoons pesto
2 tablespoons crumbled goat cheese
1 tablespoon chopped walnuts

1   Preheat the breakfast sandwich maker. Brush the polenta rounds on both sides with olive oil. Season lightly with salt and pepper on each side.

2   Place 1 polenta round in each compartment of the sandwich maker. Close and cook for 5 minutes, or until lightly browned on the underside. Remove from the sandwich maker, turn over, and spread pesto on the cooked side.

3   Place 1 polenta round in the bottom compartment, pesto side up, and sprinkle with half the goat cheese and walnuts. Lower the middle plate, then put the second polenta round in the top compartment, pesto side up, and sprinkle with the remaining goat cheese and walnuts. Close the sandwich maker.

4   Cook for 5 more minutes, until the cheese is melty and the polenta is lightly browned on the bottom. Open the sandwich maker just enough to access the bottom compartment and slide out the bottom polenta pesto round with a spatula, then slide out the middle plate to drop the top polenta down and remove it from the sandwich maker.

ZUCCHINI PARMESAN MELT

If you're planning to grill your dinner one evening, grill a few thick zucchini slices at the same time and you'll be able to have this easy meatless meal the next day. To make the slices big enough, cut the zucchini diagonally into oblongs.

Makes 1 serving

1 tablespoon extra-virgin olive oil
Kosher salt and ground black pepper
2 bias-cut zucchini slices, ½ inch thick
2 tablespoons tomato sauce
2 tablespoons grated mozzarella cheese
1 tablespoon grated Parmesan cheese

1   If you're using already-grilled zucchini, skip this step. Otherwise, heat the oil in a small nonstick pan over medium-high heat. Sprinkle salt and pepper on both sides of the zucchini slices and sauté in the hot oil until soft and lightly browned, turning halfway through, about 4 to 5 minutes total.

2   Preheat the sandwich maker.

3   Place 1 cooked zucchini slice in the bottom compartment of the heated sandwich maker. Spoon on half the tomato sauce, then sprinkle with half the mozzarella and Parmesan cheeses. Lower the middle plate.

4   Repeat the previous step with the second zucchini slice, placing it in the top compartment and topping it with the remaining tomato sauce and cheeses. Close the sandwich maker.

5   Cook for 5 minutes, or until the ingredients are heated through and the cheese is melted. Slide out the middle plate to assemble the stack and remove it from the sandwich maker.

Chapter Seven

MAKE-AHEAD COMPONENTS

The recipes in this chapter are intended to be made ahead of time, so you can use them to create your sandwiches. Make them up on the weekend or when you have a little spare time, so you'll be able to use them for quick breakfasts or other meals all week long.

BASIC BISCUITS

Make up a batch of these biscuits on the weekend and you'll have them ready for grab-and-go sandwiches during the week! To keep the size and shape uniform, I recommend investing in a muffin-top or whoopie-pie pan that has cups to fit your sandwich maker (see page 4). Otherwise, keep in mind that biscuits will expand a little as they bake, so cut them a bit smaller than the desired finished size.

Rolling the dough thin and stacking pairs of biscuits before baking will give you finished biscuits that are easy to split in half for use in sandwiches.

Makes 3 biscuits

1 tablespoon butter or cooking spray, for pans
1 cup all-purpose flour, plus more for work surface
1 teaspoon baking powder
½ teaspoon kosher salt
3 tablespoons chilled butter, cut into small pieces
½ cup cold buttermilk

1 Preheat the oven to 400°F. Grease or spray a muffin-top pan or a baking sheet.

2 In a medium bowl, combine the flour, baking powder, and salt; mix thoroughly with a fork or whisk. Add the butter, using clean hands or a pastry blender to break up the pieces and rub them into the flour. The result should be small, pea-size clumps. Add the buttermilk and use a fork to stir it into the flour mixture, just until everything is combined into a shaggy dough.

3 Turn the dough onto a lightly floured work surface and pat or roll to about a ¼-inch thickness. Use a 3½-inch biscuit cutter or a knife to cut 6 rounds.

4 Transfer the rounds to the prepared muffin-top pan or baking sheet, stacking them in pairs to make 3 biscuits. (Leave several inches between biscuits if you're using a baking sheet). Bake for 15 minutes, until lightly golden. Don't let the biscuits get too dark, as they will toast more in the sandwich maker.

Biscuit Variations

Sweet Biscuits. To the flour mixture, add 2 tablespoons sugar. If you wish, before baking the biscuits, brush with a lightly beaten egg and sprinkle with sanding sugar or turbinado sugar. Use these biscuits with sweet fillings, as for Warm Strawberry Shortcake (page 113), S'mores Toast (page 110), and Sweet Fruit Breakfast Sandwich (page 28).

Herb Biscuits. Stir ¼ cup minced fresh herbs into the buttermilk before adding it to the dough. Good herbs to use include minced chives or parsley. This recipe can be used for any savory biscuit sandwich. With mint, it would even be good for Warm Strawberry Shortcake (page 113).

Cheese Biscuits. Toss ¼ cup finely grated cheese into the dough after you incorporate the butter but before you pour in the buttermilk. The best cheeses to use for this are semi-hard or hard types such as cheddar, pepper jack, Colby, Parmesan, or Asiago. Try these cheese biscuits for any of the savory biscuit sandwiches in this book.

CORN CAKES

These little cakes are similar to cornbread, but with a sturdier, less crumbly texture, which makes them good foundations for breakfast sandwiches. Use them in place of an English muffin or in the recipe for Savory Corn Cakes with Salsa and Pepper Jack (page 25).

Makes 8 cakes, enough for 4 sandwiches

¾ cup milk (whole or low-fat)
1 large egg
2 tablespoons butter, melted and cooled, plus more for pan
1 cup all-purpose flour
1¼ cups cornmeal
1½ teaspoons baking powder
½ teaspoon kosher salt

1   Preheat the oven to 375°F. In a liquid measuring cup or small bowl, whisk together the milk, egg, and butter.

2   In a medium bowl, combine the flour, cornmeal, baking powder, and salt. Pour the liquid mixture into the dry ingredients and stir just until combined. A thick dough should form, similar to biscuit dough.

3   Grease the cups of a muffin-top or whoopie pie pan (the cups should measure around 4 inches) with butter. Scoop about ¼ cup dough into a muffin cup and pat lightly to fill the space; it should be about ½ inch thick. Repeat with the remaining dough.

4   Bake for 15 minutes, or until lightly golden. If not using right away, let cool completely before storing in a plastic bag or covered container at room temperature for up to 2 days.

BACON LATTICE PATTIES

This clever way of preparing bacon makes perfectly sized patties for many of the breakfast sandwiches in this book. Thin bacon slices without too much fat work best, rather than thick-cut butcher bacon.

Makes 2 bacon patties

4 slices bacon
Cooking spray

1   Preheat the oven to 400°F. Line a baking sheet with aluminum foil and spray lightly with cooking spray.

2   Cut the bacon slices in half crosswise to make 8 short pieces. Line up 2 pieces on the baking sheet, long edges touching. Place 2 more pieces crosswise on top of the first 2. Now "weave" the slices into a simple lattice. Lift the end of 1 bottom piece to slide the end of 1 top piece underneath, then do the same with the opposite ends of the other 2 pieces.

3   Repeat with the remaining 4 pieces of bacon to weave a second bacon "patty."

4   Bake for 20 to 25 minutes, until the bacon is crispy. Line a plate with a paper towel and use a spatula to transfer the cooked bacon patties to the plate; blot any excess oil with another paper towel. Let cool slightly before using in the breakfast sandwich of your choice. It's best to use them immediately, but they could keep, wrapped in aluminum foil and refrigerated, for up to 1 day.

BASIC PANCAKES

This pancake recipe is simple and delicious! I use it for regular breakfast pancakes and then cook up any extra batter to use in breakfast sandwiches during the week. I've included sweet and savory variations; you could divide your batter in half to make a couple different types.

Makes about 10 (4-inch) pancakes

¾ cup all-purpose flour
1 teaspoon baking powder
½ teaspoon kosher salt
2 teaspoons sugar
1 large egg
½ cup milk (whole or lowfat)
2 tablespoons butter, melted and cooled slightly
Additional butter for pan

1   In a medium bowl, combine the flour, baking powder, salt, and sugar. Stir with a whisk to combine thoroughly. In a separate bowl, whisk the egg until smooth, then whisk in the milk and 2 tablespoons butter. Pour the wet ingredients into the dry ingredients and stir with the whisk just until the dry ingredients are mixed in.

2   Heat a large griddle or nonstick skillet over medium heat. Add about 1 tablespoon butter and use a heatproof turning spatula to move it around the pan to coat completely.

3   Spoon batter into the pan to make pancakes the right size to fit a sandwich maker compartment. (A 4-inch pancake will take about 2 tablespoons of batter.) Work in batches if necessary, allowing an inch or so between pancakes. Cook for about 4 minutes, until the edges are starting to look dry and the undersides are lightly browned. Flip the pancakes over and cook about 2 minutes more, until browned on the other side.

4   Remove from the pan and let cool completely before storing in a zip-top plastic bag or plastic wrap. The pancakes will keep for 2 to 3 days either at room temperature or in the refrigerator.

Pancake Variations

Herbed Pancakes. At the end of Step 1, stir in 1 tablespoon minced fresh herbs. Good herbs to use include chives, parsley, cilantro, and basil. Use herbed pancakes in place of English muffins, or in the Herbed Pancakes with Prosciutto and Egg recipe on page 58.

Sweet Pancakes. Increase the sugar to 1 tablespoon and add ½ teaspoon vanilla to the egg-milk mixture. You can use this recipe with sweet fillings in any of the recipes, such as the Black Forest Pancake Torte (page 119). It would be great with the Sweet Egg and Waffle recipe (page 117) or the Raspberry-Nutella Stack (page 114).

BUCKWHEAT PANCAKES

I originally developed these pancakes for the Millionaire sandwich on page 52, but their hearty flavor would work well with other pancake-based sandwiches in this book, both sweet and savory. I adapted the recipe from a Russian cookbook from the 1980s called *The Art of Russian Cuisine,* by Anne Volokh. These are a little more work than traditional pancakes, since you beat the egg whites as for traditional Russian blini, but the resulting thick and fluffy pancake makes a sturdy vessel for fillings.

Makes about 12 (4-inch) pancakes

1 cup all-purpose flour
¾ cup buckwheat flour
1 tablespoon sugar
½ teaspoon kosher salt
1 teaspoon baking powder
2 large eggs, separated
¼ cup unsalted butter, melted and cooled slightly
1½ cups buttermilk
Butter or cooking spray for griddle

1 In a bowl, combine the flours, sugar, salt, and baking powder. Stir with a whisk or a fork to combine. Add the egg yolks, ¼ cup melted butter, and buttermilk; stir until well combined.

2 In a separate bowl, beat the egg whites with a handheld electric mixer on medium speed, increasing to high speed, until stiff peaks form. Scrape the whites into the batter and use a rubber spatula to fold them in until just incorporated (the batter can be a little streaky).

3 Preheat a nonstick grill or a griddle over medium heat. Lightly coat with butter or cooking spray. Spoon about ¼ cup batter onto the griddle, spreading it slightly with the back of another spoon to make a pancake about 4 inches in diameter. Repeat with more batter, allowing a couple of inches between pancakes.

4 Cook for 2 to 3 minutes, until the pancake undersides are lightly browned and the tops are starting to look dry around the edges. Flip the pancakes over and let cook for 1 to 2 minutes more, until the undersides are lightly browned. Transfer the cooked pancakes to a plate and repeat, coating the pan again with butter or cooking spray, until all the batter has been used.

5 Use the pancakes immediately or let cool, wrap tightly in plastic wrap, and refrigerate for 3 to 4 days or freeze for up to 1 month.

SUSHI RICE CAKES

Make these molded rice cakes as an unconventional vessel for your sandwiches. In the sandwich maker, the exterior of the cakes crisps up, creating a delicious handheld meal. Find sushi rice in the Asian food section of your supermarket or at an international grocery store. These rice cakes can be used for the Salmon-Rice Stack (page 75) and Tamago Egg on Sushi Cakes (page 74).

Makes 8 rice cakes

1½ cups white sushi (short-grain) rice
2 cups water
3 tablespoons unseasoned rice vinegar
1 tablespoon sugar
1 teaspoon salt

1   Place the rice in a saucepan and cover with cold water. Swish the rice around in the water, grabbing handfuls and rubbing the grains together in your hand. Drain off the water, then refill and repeat once or twice more, until the water drains nearly clear. This will help prevent the rice on the bottom of the pan from burning.

2   Drain completely and then add 2 cups water to the pan. Bring to a simmer over medium-high heat, then reduce to low and cook, covered, for 15 minutes, or until the rice is cooked through and the water is almost completely absorbed. Remove from the heat and let sit, covered and undisturbed, for 10 minutes to allow the rice to absorb the rest of the water.

3   While the rice is resting, in a small bowl combine the rice vinegar, sugar, and salt. Stir until the sugar and salt dissolve.

4   Use a fork or rice paddle to fluff the rice, then drizzle the vinegar mixture over it. Continue to fluff and turn the rice until the vinegar is mixed in completely. Let sit until cool enough to handle.

5   On a flat work surface, press a scant ½-cup scoop of rice firmly into the middle of a 4-inch round cutter to form a patty about ½ inch thick. Repeat with the remaining rice. Let the patties cool and then wrap in plastic wrap to store in the refrigerator. Use within a day; after that, the rice will begin to harden.

COOKIE CRUSTS

Craving something sweet? Whip up these little sugar-cookie crusts to use as the "bread" for a sweet sandwich. Fill them with marshmallow, chocolate, fruit, or other fillings, or use them as the base for the Warm Mini Cheesecakes on page 111.

Makes 4 (4-inch) cookie rounds

4 tablespoons unsalted butter, softened
2 tablespoons sugar
⅛ teaspoon kosher salt
½ teaspoon vanilla extract
⅔ cup all-purpose flour

1 Preheat the oven to 350°F.

2 In a small bowl, use a fork to cream together the butter, sugar, salt, and vanilla until smooth and creamy, the consistency of frosting. Add the flour, stirring just until the mixture is clumpy and no dry flour remains.

3 Divide the mixture into 4 parts. Using an ungreased muffin-top pan or whoopie pie pan with 4-inch cups, press each clump of dough into a muffin cup.

4 Bake for 10 minutes, or until the cookies are very lightly browned on the underside. Do not overcook, as they will brown a little more in the sandwich maker. Let cool completely and store in a sealed container for up to 1 week.

CARAMELIZED ONIONS

When cooked long enough, onions develop a mellow, sweet flavor that lends itself nicely to breakfast sandwiches, burgers, and other dishes. Make up a batch of these onions when you have a little time, and keep them in a container in the fridge to add a tangy-sweet element to sandwiches during the week.

Makes about ¾ cup

2 medium yellow onions
2 teaspoons extra-virgin olive oil
1 tablespoon brown sugar
Kosher salt, as needed
1 tablespoon balsamic vinegar

1   Cut the stem end off the onions, then halve lengthwise, stem to root. Remove the peel. Thinly slice the onions crosswise to make half-moon pieces, discarding the root end.

2   In a small nonstick skillet, heat the olive oil over medium-low heat. Add the onions and sprinkle with the brown sugar and a pinch of salt. Cook, stirring occasionally, until the onions soften and turn light brown, about 20 minutes.

3   Add the vinegar, stirring to combine, and cook for 5 minutes more to allow the vinegar to integrate with the onions. Remove from the heat and season to taste with additional salt. Let cool, then store in a covered container in the refrigerator for up to 1 week.

GRIT *or* POLENTA CAKES

The perfect way to use up leftover grits, polenta, or even risotto, these little cakes make a good foundation for a meal produced in the sandwich maker. Made with polenta, they can be used in place of prepared polenta in recipes like Portobello, Polenta, and Manchego Stack (page 91) and Polenta Pesto Rounds (page 94).

Makes 4 cakes

2 cups cooked grits, polenta, or risotto, cooled until thickened
Canola oil, as needed
All-purpose flour, as needed
Kosher salt and ground black pepper

1   Line a baking sheet with parchment paper and brush lightly with canola oil. Using a 4-inch round cutter as a mold, press about ½ cup cooked grits into the cutter to make a circle about ½ inch thick. Place on the prepared baking sheet. Repeat using the remaining grits to make a total of 4 cakes. (At this point, the shaped cakes can be wrapped individually in plastic wrap and refrigerated for up to 3 days.)

2   To prepare, pour enough oil into a nonstick skillet to coat the bottom; heat over medium-high heat. Unwrap the cakes, dust lightly with flour, and add to the hot pan. Cook until the undersides are crisp and browned, about 5 minutes. Use a spatula to flip the cakes over. Cook on the second side for 4 to 6 minutes, until evenly browned.

3   Sprinkle with salt and pepper and use in the recipe of your choice.

Chapter Eight

DESSERTS

Don't overlook the sweet stuff when dreaming up ways to use your sandwich maker. The recipes in this chapter make for yummy snacks when a sweet craving hits.

S'MORES TOAST

Who doesn't like the combination of toasted marshmallows and chocolate! There's no need to wait for your next camping trip when you can assemble a yummy little s'mores-inspired sandwich in your sandwich maker.

Don't skip the step of buttering the plate; it keeps the marshmallows from sticking.

Makes 1 sandwich

Butter, as needed
2 slices raisin bread, lightly toasted
2 miniature milk chocolate bars (about 1 ounce total)
2 marshmallows or ⅓ cup miniature marshmallows

1 Rub the bottom of the top compartment lightly with a bit of butter, then preheat the sandwich maker.

2 Using a 4-inch biscuit cutter or a knife, cut the raisin bread into rounds to fit the sandwich maker.

3 Place 1 bread round in the bottom compartment of the heated sandwich maker; arrange the chocolate on top of it. Lower the middle plate.

4 Place the marshmallows in the buttered top compartment. Add the second toast round. Close the sandwich maker, pressing the top down lightly if it doesn't close completely.

5 Cook for 1 minute. Slide out the middle plate to combine the s'mores components, then remove the sandwich and turn it over onto a plate so the chocolate is on top of the marshmallows.

WARM MINI CHEESECAKES

When the craving strikes but you don't want to go to the effort of making a full-size cheesecake, this mini version will do the trick. Cooked on a sweet cookie crust, the creamy filling is especially good served warm. Be sure to use only the top compartment of the sandwich maker—the bottom one doesn't get hot enough to cook the cheesecake filling.

Makes 2 cheesecakes

½ cup (4 ounces) cream cheese, softened
¼ cup sugar
½ teaspoon vanilla extract
1 large egg yolk
2 Cookie Crusts (recipe on page 106)
½ cup fresh berries (such as strawberries, raspberries, or blueberries)

1   Preheat the breakfast sandwich maker. In a small bowl, combine the cream cheese, sugar, vanilla, and egg yolk. Stir with a fork until smooth and creamy.

2   Place 1 cookie crust in the top compartment of the heated sandwich maker. Spoon half the cream cheese mixture over the crust, spreading it into an even layer. Close the sandwich maker.

3   Cook for 7 minutes. The cheesecake mixture will be thickened but still creamy. Lift the lid (some cheesecake mixture may stick to the lid; this can be scraped off and discarded), unplug the sandwich maker, and let sit for 10 minutes. Use an offset spatula to loosen the cheesecake from the sides of the sandwich maker and lift it out onto a dessert plate. Cover loosely with aluminum foil to keep warm while the other cake cooks.

4   Repeat with the remaining cookie and cream cheese mixture to make a second cheesecake.

5   To serve, top the cheesecakes with the fresh berries.

CARAMEL *and* PINEAPPLE *on* TOASTED POUND CAKE

Want to dress up a store-bought pound cake? Use a couple of slices to sandwich together warm pineapple smothered in caramel. You'll probably need to eat this with a fork, so you might as well adorn the top with a big dollop of whipped cream.

Makes 1 sandwich

2 slices pound cake, about ½ inch thick
1 tablespoon caramel sauce
1 pineapple ring, canned or fresh
Whipped cream for garnish (optional)

1 Preheat the breakfast sandwich maker. Using a 4-inch round cutter or a knife, cut the cake slices into circles to fit the sandwich maker.

2 Place 1 cake slice in the bottom compartment of the heated sandwich maker and drizzle with the caramel sauce. Lower the middle plate.

3 Place the pineapple ring in the top compartment. Close the sandwich maker.

4 Cook for 2 to 3 minutes, or until the pineapple is warm and the pound cake is lightly toasted. (Be careful—it has a high butter content, so it can burn quickly.) Slide open the middle plate to assemble the sandwich and remove it from the sandwich maker. Invert onto a plate, let cool a moment, and then top with whipped cream, if desired.

WARM STRAWBERRY SHORTCAKE

Strawberries. Biscuit. Whipped cream. It's a classic combination, and you can make a delicious version in your sandwich maker. The heat turns the strawberries soft and juicy as it warms up the biscuit.

Makes 1 serving

1 Sweet Biscuit (recipe on page 98)
½ cup halved or quartered fresh strawberries
¼ teaspoon sugar
¼ cup whipped cream

1   Preheat the breakfast sandwich maker.

2   Place the biscuit in the bottom compartment of the heated sandwich maker. Lower the middle plate.

3   Place the strawberries in the top compartment and sprinkle with the sugar. Close the sandwich maker.

4   Cook for 3 minutes, or until the strawberries are slightly softened and juicy. Slide open the middle plate to drop the strawberries onto the biscuit. Remove from the sandwich maker, spooning any strawberries that have fallen off back onto the biscuit. Top with the whipped cream.

RASPBERRY-NUTELLA STACK

Jumbo sugar cookies are the basis for this lusciously warm and gooey dessert. Use fresh raspberries for the best results, although thawed frozen berries will also work.

Makes 1 serving

2 tablespoons chocolate-hazelnut spread (such as Nutella)
2 large sugar cookies or 2 Cookie Crusts (recipe on page 106)
¼ cup fresh raspberries

1   Preheat the breakfast sandwich maker. Spread the chocolate-hazelnut spread on the undersides of the cookies.

2   Place 1 cookie, chocolate side up, in the bottom compartment of the sandwich maker. Arrange the raspberries on the cookie and then top with the second cookie, chocolate side down. Close the sandwich maker, pressing lightly to compact the sandwich and crush the berries a little.

3   Cook for 4 to 5 minutes, until the berries are soft and juicy. Open the sandwich maker and remove the cookie stack.

GOAT CHEESE *and* FIG CROISSANT

When figs are in season, this is a favorite market-fresh treat. At my farmer's market, I can pick up every ingredient I need: local honey, goat cheese from our neighborhood cheesemaker, a croissant from a nearby bakery—and the figs, of course.

Makes 1 sandwich

1 croissant
1 ounce goat cheese
2 teaspoons honey
2 fresh figs, cut into quarters

1   Preheat the breakfast sandwich maker. Using a round cutter or a knife, trim the croissant to fit the sandwich maker; split it in half.

2   Place the bottom half of the croissant in the bottom compartment of the preheated sandwich maker, cut side up. Top with the goat cheese and drizzle with the honey. Close the middle plate.

3   Arrange the figs in the top compartment of the sandwich maker. Cover with the top half of the croissant, cut side down. Close the sandwich maker (it might not close all the way, which is fine).

4   Cook for 5 minutes, or until the figs soften. Slide open the middle plate to assemble the sandwich and remove it from the sandwich maker.

APPLE PIE DONUT SANDWICH

Yes, it's a sandwich, but you'll probably need a fork to eat this creation! I love to serve it for dessert with a dollop of vanilla ice cream nestled in the center of the donut—heaven. If you can't find cider donuts, you can use a cinnamon-sugar cake donut instead.

Makes 1 sandwich

1 apple cider donut, split in half
¼ cup apple pie filling
1 tablespoon caramel sauce

1   Preheat the breakfast sandwich maker.

2   Place the bottom half of the donut in the bottom compartment of the sandwich maker, cut side up, and top with the pie filling. Close the middle plate.

3   Place the top half of the donut in the top compartment, cut side down. Close the sandwich maker.

4   Cook for 5 minutes, or until the pie filling is warm. Carefully open the sandwich maker and drizzle the caramel sauce over the pie filling in the bottom compartment. Close the sandwich maker; slide out the middle plate to assemble the sandwich and remove it from the sandwich maker.

SWEET EGG *and* WAFFLE

Custardy and comforting, this is a snack my daughters request on cold nights, or when they're feeling in need of a little TLC.

Makes 1 serving

1 large egg
1 tablespoon heavy cream
1 tablespoon sugar
⅛ teaspoon ground cinnamon
¼ teaspoon vanilla extract
2 frozen waffles, lightly toasted

1   Preheat the breakfast sandwich maker. In a small bowl, whisk together the egg, cream, sugar, cinnamon, and vanilla until smooth.

2   Place a waffle in the bottom compartment of the heated sandwich maker. Close the middle plate.

3   Pour the egg mixture into the top compartment. Close the sandwich maker.

4   Cook for 5 minutes, or until the egg is cooked through. Slide open the middle plate to drop the egg onto the waffle; remove from the sandwich maker and top with the second toasted waffle.

CHOCOLATELY BANANA *and* ALMOND STACK

Banana fans will love this dessert, which combines almond butter, warm bananas, and chocolate! I like to use a sugar cookie as a base, but a pancake or frozen waffle also works.

Makes 1 serving

1 tablespoon almond butter
1 large sugar cookie or 1 Cookie Crust (recipe on page 106)
1 banana
1 tablespoon chocolate sauce

1   Preheat the breakfast sandwich maker. Spread the almond butter over the sugar cookie. Cut the banana in half crosswise and then split each half lengthwise.

2   Put the sugar cookie, almond butter side up, in the bottom compartment of the heated sandwich maker. Lower the middle plate.

3   Arrange the banana pieces, cut side down, to fill the top compartment, reserving extra banana pieces for another use. Drizzle with the chocolate sauce. Close the sandwich maker.

4   Cook for 4 to 5 minutes, or until the banana pieces are heated through and beginning to soften. Slide open the middle plate to drop the banana onto the sugar cookie and remove it from the sandwich maker.

BLACK FOREST PANCAKE TORTE

The origin of black forest cake isn't surprising—it comes from an area of southwestern Germany known for its dark chocolate and cherries. The torte is usually an elaborate confection of liqueur-soaked sponge cake, whipped cream, cherries, and shaved chocolate, but I've whittled it down to its essence so you can enjoy this flavor combination in less than 5 minutes. If you're cooking the pancakes specifically for this recipe, sprinkle on some of the chocolate chips right after you pour the batter onto the griddle.

Makes 1 serving

½ cup cherry pie filling
¼ cup dark chocolate chips
2 (4-inch) Sweet Pancakes (recipe on page 103)
2 tablespoons whipped cream
1 tablespoon grated dark chocolate, for garnish

1 Preheat the breakfast sandwich maker. In a small bowl, stir together the pie filling and the chocolate chips.

2 Place 1 pancake in the bottom compartment of the heated sandwich maker. Spoon on half the pie filling. Lower the middle plate.

3 Place the second pancake in the top compartment and spoon on the remaining pie filling.

4 Cook for 3 to 5 minutes, until the pie filling is heated through and the chocolate chips are beginning to melt. Slide open the middle compartment to assemble the torte and transfer it from the sandwich maker to a plate. Let cool slightly, then top with the whipped cream and grated dark chocolate.

IMPROV PAIN AU CHOCOLATE

Use the best-quality chocolate bar and the freshest croissant you can find for this super-easy snack or dessert. A thin piece of chocolate from a chocolate bar works better than a thick block of baking chocolate. Add a café au lait and imagine you're in a Parisian café.

Makes 1 serving

1 mini croissant, or 1 regular croissant cut to fit the sandwich maker
1 (ounce) piece of dark chocolate

1   Preheat the breakfast sandwich maker. Split the croissant.

2   Place the bottom part of the croissant in the bottom compartment of the heated sandwich maker, cut side up. Arrange the chocolate on top. Lower the middle plate.

3   Place the other half of the croissant in the top compartment, cut side down. Close the sandwich maker.

4   Cook for 1 to 2 minutes, until the chocolate begins to melt and the croissant is warm—watch carefully to keep it from burning. Slide out the middle plate to drop the top of the croissant onto the bottom half; remove from the sandwich maker.

USEFUL CONVERSIONS

U.S. MEASURE	EQUIVALENT	METRIC
1 teaspoon	—	5 milliliters
1 tablespoon	3 teaspoons	15 milliliters
1 cup	16 tablespoons	240 milliliters
1 pint	2 cups	470 milliliters
1 quart	4 cups	950 milliliters
1 liter	4 cups + 3½ tablespoons	1000 milliliters
1 ounce (dry)	2 tablespoons	28 grams
1 pound	16 ounces	450 grams
2.21 pounds	35.3 ounces	1 kilogram

VOLUME CONVERSIONS

U.S. MEASURE	EQUIVALENT	METRIC
1 tablespoon	½ fluid ounce	15 milliliters
¼ cup	2 fluid ounces	60 milliliters
⅓ cup	3 fluid ounces	90 milliliters
½ cup	4 fluid ounces	120 milliliters
⅔ cup	5 fluid ounces	150 milliliters
¾ cup	6 fluid ounces	180 milliliters
1 cup	8 fluid ounces	240 milliliters
2 cups	16 fluid ounces	480 milliliters

WEIGHT CONVERSIONS

U.S. MEASURE	METRIC
1 ounce	30 grams
⅓ pound	150 grams
½ pound	225 grams
1 pound	450 grams

Recipe Index

Acknowledgments

This book would not be possible without the tireless support, myriad ideas, and honest feedback of my husband, Chip Harlan. I'm also grateful for my daughters, Sadie and Gillian, who are my biggest fans and most eager taste-testers. My friends and extended family are a constant source of inspiration, and I truly value their support and interest in my work. And finally, I thank Kelly Reed, Kourtney Joy, Keith Riegert, Alice Riegert, and the rest of the Ulysses Press team, who have made every book I've done with them a true pleasure.

About the Author

Jessica Goldbogen Harlan is a seasoned food writer and recipe developer. A graduate of the Institute of Culinary Education in New York, she has developed recipes for well-known food brands and magazines, interviewed celebrity chefs, judged food competitions, catered parties, and taught cooking classes. Her work has appeared in *Clean Eating, Town & Country, Pilates Style*, About.com, and Gaiam.com. This is her fifth cookbook. The previous books, all published by Ulysses Press, include *Ramen to the Rescue, Tortillas to the Rescue, Homemade Condiments,* and *Quinoa Cuisine* (co-written with Kelley Sparwasser). She lives in Atlanta, Georgia, with her husband and two daughters.